AF505070

NAi Publishers intend the Reflect series to focus attention on socially relevant themes for architecture, urban planning, fine art and design.

reflect
#01

NAi Publishers

New commitment

In architecture, art and design

4

As both 'commitment' and 'engagement' can be used in English for the very specific Dutch word 'engagement', the editor has decided to respect the well-considered choices of the individual translators.

Foreword

Simon Franke
Director NAi Publishers

Perhaps it is a general social phenomenon and comes as a reaction to a period of unprecedented economic prosperity and relative stability in international relations; perhaps it is the product of the disciplines themselves; however that may be, there is a growing discussion of social issues in architecture, urban planning, fine art, photography and design. Architects, designers and artists are searching for the legitimation of their work and for activities that are relevant to society. The specialist journals call for reflection and reappraisal of professional practice. In other words, a debate is clearly getting under way on a new form of commitment to current social problems on the part of the design and visual disciplines. Unlike what seems to have happened in the 1960s and 1970s, this commitment is barely linked to political debates that are intended to yield a dominant ideology. This interest in society finds expression in the most diverse forms, such as social scientific research on urbanism in order to influence the practice of urban design, or a different design practice in which specific project designs and works of art (as well as reflection on them) often show signs of an interdisciplinary approach. And of course (especially in fine art) there is a theoretical, intellectual discourse in which discussion takes place on coming to terms with shocking events like the two attacks on the World Trade Center on 11 September 2001.

Perceptions like these have also percolated to our publishing house during the last few years. For NAi Publishers, discussions with critics, architects and artists have never been purely about technical production, but have also had a strong substantial component. The conclusion of this is *Reflect*, an initiative for a new and varied series of very different books, books without *partis-pris*, books in which theory and practice are of equal weight, books both topical and historical. They are all books in which the text predominates over the images, aimed at a broad professional audience from very different disciplines and at the interested non-specialist, intended to influence the debate and public opinion. We view the tenth anniversary of NAi Publishers as the moment to launch the first volume of the series.

For the collection of essays *New Commitment*, the first volume in the series *Reflect*, NAi Publishers and NAi Booksellers invited some thirty authors to contribute. Many of them are among our permanent contacts; they are the authors of publications that we have produced in the last few years, the very contacts that inspired us to come up with this new series. Others were invited because we were convinced that they could make an interesting contribution to this collection of essays. We asked ten authors, mainly from the circles of academics and critics, to submit somewhat longer contributions on a theme proposed by us. Their *Reflections* provide the book with a structure, as well as a diversity that does full justice to the subject. In addition, a number of authors were asked to write a short piece on a subject of their choice, the statement of a position, often connected with experiences in the everyday practice in which these authors operate. These have become the *Positions*. *Reflections* and *Positions* can be distinguished in the book by the different typographies. Some *Positions*, however, have become *Reflections*, and above all there are a good many *Positions* that can be recognised in the *Reflections*. What else could we have expected?

Commitment is difficult, so much becomes clear after reading the articles in this book; much more difficult than in the past, that is, in the 1960s and 1970s. At that time social commitment was a part of political movements with a corresponding ideology. The 'task' of the artist, architect or designer was a logical consequence of that. Several authors in this collection are afraid that the new commitment may turn out to be 'old commitment'. They call the importance of the topic into question and are above all afraid that the autonomy of the artist may be eroded. Others, especially those writing on architecture, regard a new commitment as meaningful in a reappraisal of today's design challenges. There can be no doubt about the fact that commitment as we knew it thirty years ago is out of the question. But sometimes it also looks as though there is no clear-cut topic of debate at all, and thus no new commitment either. Still, there are various phenomena in society that can be interpreted in a different way, and the authors in this collection display a high level of involvement in social problems and in the determination of the position of the architect, artist and designer, without their articles heading in the same direction at all. That diversity is certainly a first improvement on the old commitment.

Finally, it is good for us to realize that commitment, as described by René Boomkens in the opening article, does not exist by

virtue of the radical, individual choice and the corresponding act
of resistance, but depends on the 'enthusiasm of the bystander'.
'Engagement is not an individual choice, but the expression of
collective commitment in a crucial movement or development.'
The editors of this publication hope that this collection of essays
will make a contribution to that collective involvement.

Contents

Engagement *after* progress

New commitment

I wanna do right, but not right now.
Gillian Welch

I need a crowd of people,
But I can't face them day to day.
Though my problems are meaningless,
That don't make them go away.
Neil Young

1   'You're either with us or against us.'

A paradigm shift in the cultural climate had already been
underway for years, a move away from postmodern relativism
and artistic navel-staring towards diverse artistic expressions
which were presented as a 'statement', from the laconic pronouncement of writer Dave Eggers that irony had become passé
or the novels of his colleague Michel Houellebecq which read
like vicious attacks on the prevailing order to the most recent
edition of the *Documenta* in Kassel where, according to many
commentators, the art was well-nigh buried beneath political
statements. It is impossible to enumerate all the exhibitions
with an explicitly political tone since then. Especially since the
attacks on the Twin Towers and the Pentagon, it has become
impossible for the arts to avoid accounting for their social role
and political significance. This has only been exacerbated by the
worldwide conflict between the US (i.e. the West) and various
Islamic revival and terror movements being described by all
parties as a prime example of a *cultural* conflict, a conflict
which is not just about economic interests or political power
but about clashing worldviews and ways of life. A few years ago,
the American historian Samuel Huntington even talked about
a looming 'clash of civilizations' on a global scale, and he was
also primarily referring to the portentous conflict between
modern Western culture and the Islamic world. Modernity
itself was at stake. That is a quite different drum to the one we
could hear being sounded by Francis Fukuyama some 14 years
ago. In his controversial essay *The End of History*, published
just before the fall of the Berlin Wall, he concluded that political and economic liberalism had triumphed worldwide and that
the fundamentalist revival at that time (Christian and Jewish
but primarily, of course, of Islamic ilk) would not result in much

more than some rearguard actions. No, the triumphal march of liberalism meant nothing less than the end of history, which is about the same thing as the end of ideologies, which sociologist Daniel Bell already talked about in the 1960s, or the end of the 'meta-narrative', a term which was already the catchphrase in literary and architectural circles in the 1960s and for which we owe thanks to Jean-François Lyotard, the man who gave us a philosophical interpretation of postmodernism. Fukuyama was, moreover, not overly triumphal about the victory of liberalism, concluding his essay in a rather sombre mood with the lament that after the victory we have been left with an unmistakable sense of melancholy or boredom. Could it be more in keeping with the dominant mood in the West towards the end of the 1980s? Jeff Koons had just treated us to his painted polychrome pig *Ushering into Banality*, the world had just been exposed to Bret Easton Ellis's *Less than zero*, in which the highlights of day-to-day existence for the cocaine-snorting characters include watching snuff movies and mutual masturbation due to a lack of true lust. There was a controversial exhibition in New York of so-called *deconstructivist* architects, who were nominally extremely critical yet confronted the public with buildings which first of all seemed to be meant to implode and displayed their fragmentedness like a self-assured admission of their failure. What irony! Pride in one's own impotence as a unique selling point. Meanwhile, the new 'house' culture was shuttling between Chicago, Detroit, London and Munich, providing the radical individualism and hedonism of about 30 years of pop and mass culture with a new choreography: the never-ending ecstasy of dance as the ultimate form of collectivity and solidarity of individuals who had not even one jot of memory of such notions. Some people called it 'dancing on the edge of the volcano', as if to attribute a deeper meaning to house. In fact there was nobody still interested in hearing about deeper meanings; postmodernism was pre-eminently an attitude to life and a world-view that thrived on superficies. Bigger connections, deeper layers – it was all swapped for a light-footed identification with the ephemeral, coincidental, temporary: Plato definitively beaten by the sophists; philosophy and politics by the rapidly mutating reality of trendwatchers, spin doctors and marketeers. The welfare state, the showpiece of half a century of political struggle and planning and a comprehensive vision of state, society and individual, crumbled away in favour of the anarchy and fickleness of the free market, and Margaret Thatcher became (in)famous for her statement that there is no such thing as society.

Postmodernism was certainly liberating – it not only put paid to stick-in-the-mud and obsolete ideologies and to the false profundity of all-embracing philosophies, but also to the general acceptance of modern forms of authority, such as that of the academic, the technocrat, the bureaucrat. Postmodernism was closely linked to the 'do-it-yourself' attitude so typical of the punk subculture of the late 1970s. That attitude concentrated on the tangibility of the immediate living environment, the personal world of experience of individuals who harboured a deep distrust of any attempt to make statements about bigger contexts or connections. Distrusting every universalism as a veiled attempt at oppression or exclusion of marginal, deviant or unusual identities, punk and postmodernism opted for a simultaneously militant and playful particularism, which happily traded in the achievements of the welfare state for that of the playground, the amusement park and the video game, though preferably with retention of unemployment benefit. Sure, that is a cheap swipe, but it does touch on a crucial problem of the sometimes ever so liberating postmodernism: the inability to account for the conditions or roots of individual freedom and licentiousness, the sense of relentless impermanence and an inexhaustible series of possible choices, and the implicit sense of arbitrariness, coincidence and openness. Postmodernism is generous: as an ethos and worldview which belong to a post-Fordian and flexible service- and experience-based economy and consumer society it wants everyone to share in the abundance, the pleasure and the freedom. Come and join in, there is plenty of room! The main thing is to do your own thing: long live the multicultural and polymorphously perverse society in which all identities are interchangeable and exchangeable, but make sure you do it yourself! However, you cannot claim that identity does not exist, that everything is relative and nothing certain, that our 'ego' is a 19th-century illusion, while simultaneously demanding that everyone has to do it all for themselves, that personal initiative is everything. 'Ego' and 'persona' are fictions and, moreover, are fluid, relative and unstable. Postmodernists understand the everyday mood of recent decades perfectly: who or what we are is indeed instable, to a large degree fictitious and fragmentary, inconstant and untrustworthy, we are products of familial, political, scientific, technological and communications media and interrelationships, of complex bureaucracies, market forces, care organizations and so on. Yet those who reach this conclusion make themselves ridiculous if they think that we can best take on the world with a light-hearted and optimistic attitude of 'do-it-yourself". Everything that you yourself would want to undertake was decided long ago, was contrived by others, scientifically tested and statistically checked. Your favourite chair was designed by IKEA, and that explains why Fukuyama, at least at the end of his essay, briefly drops his guard and associates liberalism's great victory with ennui. Postmodernism is similar to liberalism, but then without personal initiative, without the autonomous individual, without personal identity. Without ever intending it, this is how postmodernism has become the evil conscience of liberalism. Postmodernism alerted us to the fact that the autonomy and freedom of the subject is a *construction*, a *fabrication*, a fiction, though indeed a 'real fiction', just as other aspects of our identity are 'real fictions', such as our nationality, our citizenship, and even our sexual identity.

Doubts about and the modification of fundamentals, grass roots, of the stability of our identity, of the realness of our experience and world of experience, the fear-inducing yet stimulating feeling of living in a simulated reality, a *hyper-reality* that luxuriated in excess and ecstasy, that in postmodernism everything is pushed to the limit, sometimes in a playful, ironic manner but more often in a cynical, illusionless one, and finally also in a way that mercilessly undermined one's personal intellectual or artistic contribution. Postmodern art that thematized the boredom, the lack of identity (or indeed the excess of identities), soon became boring and identityless itself – and the later work of, for example, Jeff Koons clearly suffered from this. Art which made a pastiche both of and based on elements from popular (media) culture constantly risked being unable to make any difference to that mass culture. At the same time it did not suffer from it, since it had now become a postmodern rule of thumb *par excellence* to be more banal than the banality of which you were making a pastiche. In the footsteps of the sometimes deeply moving and gripping novels by Bret Easton Ellis about boredom, lack of identity, anonymity and (imaginary) extreme violence, readers were confronted with a flood of hundreds of other novels about the same, preferably even cruder, even more roughshod, even more frank, even 'more boring'. The pastiches of pornographic or extremely violent literature were bound to prompt all kinds of ethical discussions among 'true' literati. This also transpired in the world of (fashion) photography, where the same themes filtered through, in the world of film, where the *nouvelle violence* (note the studied, arty branding of this *American* genre) of Quentin Tarantino and others briefly gained a following, and in pop music, where the explicit references to violence, rape and crime in 'gangsta rap' led to a true post-modernization of the American justice system: lawyers had to explain that the aggressive language of the rappers had nothing to do with reality or, therefore, with real intentions, but that it was an artistic convention or construct which was closely linked with the everyday, banal patois in the black ghettos. And the rappers were consistently acquitted!

However, the ethical discussions and judicial procedures obscured the black hole at the heart of the postmodern attitude to life and artistic practice, in which every ethical standpoint, cultural criticism or political position evaporated at the speed of light: the black hole of the fundamental lack of seriousness that attached to postmodernism. That frivolity was once applied as an antidote to the Calvinistic self-denial of modernism (by architecture historian Charles Jencks, for example) or to the ideological iron discipline of Marxism (by Jean-François Lyotard), but after more than a decade of postmodernism it had lost its critical impetus. Frivolity suddenly became terribly tedious. Some postmodernists and intellectuals or artists who were associated with postmodernism underwent a remarkable 'conversion' in the course of the 1990s. Putting the new or per-ceived 'new' phenomenon of *globalization* on the agenda, which primarily manifested itself in the rise of new communication and information media and in the intensification and globaliza-tion of streams of migration, induced many people to abandon the postmodern agenda, exchanging the 'little narratives' for a new universalism, or for new *engagement*, for new 'seriousness'. Big questions and big controversies seemed to redeem the thousands of blooming flowers of the postmodern 'differences' (the small, meaningless distinctions). Jacques Derrida was the champion of so-called deconstructivism in philosophy, a style of thinking primarily designed to debunk the uncommunicative-ness and quasi-universal character of 'grand' philosophies and to catch them out on their inconsistencies and 'slips of the tongue'. In the 1990s, he suddenly showed himself to be a thinker who applied himself to serious political and ethical questions, such as the heritage of Marxism, the significance of the urban public sphere as a sanctuary for migrants, refugees and the like. In the mid-1990s, his colleague Richard Rorty, who had once protested in faultless postmodern fashion that philosophy is nothing but one literary genre among many others, abruptly turned his attention to his academic colleagues in the human-ities, and most especially to the typically postmodern practi-tioners of the new interdisciplinary field of 'cultural studies'. He appealed to them to at last call a halt to all that postmodern navel-staring and all that debate about cultural identity and difference, and instead to demonstrate *engagement* with the *truly serious* social and political issues. Rorty was primarily referring to the gargantuan social divide and poverty in the US and the threat of societal disruption that it spawns. Rorty's call to arms was published as *Achieving Our Country*, and this title betrayed an obvious post-postmodern agenda, albeit in a form that was far from unproblematic. 'Let us achieve our country, fulfil its promise,' Rorty seems to call out to his intellectual compatriots – and with 'country' he means above all the political and social ideals couched in the American constitution. Rorty endeavours to formulate a new collective ideal, or to breathe new life into an old collective ideal, against the prevailing tendency of postmodern individualism and thinking in terms of difference. He then strides fearlessly into battle against, for example, American novelists who say really unpleasant things about the US, such as writing that America is not a nation of free and equal individuals at all, but the product of a worldwide conspiracy of multinationals. Let us just say that *engagement* is difficult.

However, it has made a comeback. At least it seems to have made a comeback: engagement, new seriousness. There is a renewed commitment to issues and problems that have an evident *collective* if not *universal* character: poverty, social and cultural exclusion, economic exploitation, political and ideological vio-lence. In the late 1970s and early 1980s, most of these terms disappeared in the paper shredder of the New Free-Market Economy, 'deregulation' and the gradual cutting back of the great social-democratic structure of the welfare state which in recent years, thanks in part to the social democrats themselves, seems to have reached its zenith. Since then, the babyboomers, now ageing, have been complaining about the inability or unwilling-ness of younger generations to take up the torch of criticism, resistance and rebellion. But these younger generations no longer stand for being lectured by worn-out revolutionaries who themselves have ended up in comfortable positions of power in the world of politics, culture or the media. The label 'Generation X' (in the Netherlands bastardized to '*Generatie Nix*' – 'Generation Nothing') was not stuck on the generation that grew up in the 1980s by critical or now-cynical ex-rebels, but by a companion in distress and a contemporary, the novelist Douglas Coupland. Rather than wanting to express anonymity, identitylessness or resignation with this label, he above all wished to outline the altered circumstances in which his gener-ation grew up. His characters are by no means empty-headed

or solipsistic, instead being almost overly aware of the cultural
given that age-old general perspectives on change, emancipation
or self-fulfilment (the dreams of the Sixties) are no longer a given
and have been replaced by a more or less fragmented and directionless (aimless) cultural universe, a world without many
anchoring points where they must establish their own place. It
is a completely different challenge to the one faced by the very
young babyboomers in the 1960s. Before we can answer the
question of whether we can indeed ascertain something like a
growing commitment or engagement with more general political
or social issues and problems in recent years – especially in
artistic and intellectual circles and practices – it is useful to
think back once again to that wonderful era of engagement and
resistance against the prevailing political and cultural order,
the curious and 'unique' Sixties and their aftermath. The fact
that we are currently talking about a 'revival' in engagement,
reveals in and of itself the relationship that we evidently still
entertain with that period.

2   The beach beneath the asphalt

According to many people, the last massive surge in popular
resistance and 'engagement' with the future of the world and
humanity was in what is now called 'the Sixties', an epoch of
confusion and ideological unrest, of waves of emancipation in
all kinds of areas, and an era that some people described as the
'last phase of the Enlightenment'. Although we can read the
adjective 'last' in various ways (as the 'newest', but also as the
'ultimate' or 'final', and also perhaps as the most 'outdated'),
in all these cases these critical voices have proven to be right:
almost 40 years later, it is still the newest, the ultimate and the
most outdated variant of the Enlightenment. Here in 2003,
terms like emancipation, liberation, revolution, rebellion and
popular resistance are still associated with the 1960s, which
actually started somewhere in 1964 and continued through
1975 at least, around the time of the Carnation Revolution in
Portugal and the end of the Vietnam War. Thereafter, it was
over with the optimism, the naivety, the dreaminess and the
sentimentality, and not to be forgotten, the sometimes kitschy
religiosity and the unparalleled and unthinking creativity of
more than a decade of 'Enlightenment'. None of this has
returned, not even in the cheerful 1990s, which began with the
end of Communism and the fall of the Berlin Wall in 1989. This
decade was stoked up even more by the introduction of the new
and highly promising communication medium of the Internet
in 1991. Briefly, *very briefly*, it seemed to be the dawn of a

new period of Enlightenment. Never mind. The demise of the Communist regimes felt more like some kind of *return* to the bosom of democracy and liberalism rather than some form of progress, and the Internet Revolution soon turned out to be primarily a development that was commercially lucrative rather than the hoped-for new phase of democratization and universal communication. In addition, it was brutally spun off course by the Gulf War, during which progress was primarily associated with 'precision bombing' and technological and clinical tactics, as well as with a 'new world order' proclaimed by the leaders of the old order. More than a decade later, we truly seem to be living under the new world order which was set out during the Gulf War and defined accordingly – in military and imperialistic terms. It employs phrases such as pre-emptive strike, preventive action, war against terror, the clash of civilizations, the axis of evil and rogue states.

On the face of it, 2003 seems to have nothing in common with 1968. Initially, 2003 brings to mind suicide attacks in Jerusalem and the American suppression of terrorism in Iraq, while we associate 1968 with the longing for the beach that must lie hidden beneath the asphalt of big cities. The fairytale metaphor of a hard and extremely modern material like asphalt that holds such a natural and liberating reality as that of the beach within or under it seems like a joke under the current circumstances. Nevertheless, there are more similarities between the rebellious 1960s and the current age than it might seem at first. Then as well, a chaotic and extremely destructive war of the US against 'the empire of evil' was a crucial component of the global political context in which the rebellion developed. There is good reason for 'Vietnam' currently serving as material for comparison and a reference point for a range of views about the war which the US is waging against 'international terrorism'. The protests against the Vietnam War were motivated by what was then termed 'engagement' – with the Third World, with decolonization or with socialism. The massive protest movement was supported, and in many instances led, by artists and intellectuals who manned the barricades like full-blooded activists, waved flags and distributed pamphlets – against war or the 'military-industrial complex', for peace, socialism and democratization. Artists such as Bob Dylan, Allan Greenberg and Frederic Wiseman, intellectuals such as Susan Sontag, Noam Chomsky, Bertrand Russell, Jean-Paul Sartre and Michel Foucault, were involved in the resistance and operated as the principal interpreters and mouthpieces of the rebellion.

The labelling of this artistic and intellectual civil disobedience
as 'engagement' was due to a large extent to the philosophical
movement of *existentialism*, which was influential and popular
in those days and was primarily propounded by philosophers
and writers like Sartre, Simone de Beauvoir and Albert Camus.
Engagement was seen as the product of an authentic and free
choice, taken by an autonomous individual who rejects his
mauvaise foi, in other words his dependence on prevailing
opinion, on the views of the majority. By breaking with the
conformism and the facility of a calm and anonymous life as a
herd animal, the individual can succeed in achieving his or her
autonomy, gaining and realizing his or her freedom. In turn,
that freedom does not allow itself to be founded any further: it
exists in and as the deed, the choice to take control of one's own
life. Existentialism was initially associated with radical individualism, which placed all the emphasis on life being finite
and the absurdity of human existence, which is brief, brutal
and without sense. The free choice of the individual coincided
with the heroic affirmation of that finiteness and absurdity.
It was Camus in particular who remained true to this strict,
dramatic variant of existentialism, while Sartre and De
Beauvoir started to link individual autonomy with the freedom
struggle of others – also in the collective sense – with ever-
greater emphasis. This engagement was philosophically legitim-
ated by an identification with anyone who took responsibility
for his or her personal fate, but it remained a wobbly legitimacy,
simply because existentialism had always placed the emphasis
on the fundamental uniqueness and solitude of the individual,
who has nothing but his or her own mortal body and can only
give meaning to his or her own mortality on this basis. This
ambiguity, which was associated with the engagement of the
existentialists, partly explains the fairly irresponsible and
random radicalism that was often associated with it. At the
height of his philosophical and activist fame, Sartre was a highly
controversial figure. He was not only at loggerheads with his
former friend Camus, but also had to bear the brunt of cutting
criticism of his sometimes extremely odd choices and forms
of engagement, including his well-nigh uncritical attitude
towards the Soviet Union, his almost aesthetically motivated
defence of revolutionary violence in the struggle against
colonialism in the foreword to the celebrated *Les damnés de la
terre* by the Algerian author Frantz Fanon – liberation comes
from the barrel of a gun and a dead colonial is a double liberation:
the liberation of the slave, who no longer has a master, and the
liberation of the colonial himself, who is dead now – and lastly,

his visit to the 'terrorists' of the *Rote Armee Fraktion* in prison in Germany.

To sum it up, there was something arbitrary in the existentialistically motivated *engagement*, for the very reason that it was difficult to establish a credible link between the radical individualism which it underlay and the commitment to the fate, the interests or the struggle of others. This problem applied more generally for many forms of resistance and activism which arose in the 1960s and '70s, from the unpredictable and directionless actions of the so-called situationists protesting against the automatisms of consumer society to the 'happenings' staged by the Provo movement in the Netherlands, which had a 'playful' and deliberately non-serious character, or the 'love-ins' of the hippies, which seemed more like parties than true acts of resistance. The whole idea of *engagement* had, in other words, a rather aesthetic motivation and can, with hindsight, best be characterized as a typical artist ideology. It was not the substance of the rebellion or the resistance that counted most, but the rebellion or the act of resistance itself. Resisting, rebelling, being mutinous did not need to be externally motivated, prompted by the observation of one form of injustice or another, but was commendable in and of itself. 'Living is rebelling' was the typical adolescent stance of many activists, who simply dissociated themselves from 'the' authorities and 'the' majority or, as the members of the Provo movement in the Netherlands put it, the 'hoi polloi'. The only political ideology that corresponded with this aesthetics of resistance was that of anarchism, which was perfectly aligned with the radical individualism that predominated the rebellion. Artists did not need to explain or legitimate their rebellion beyond that; they merely had to demonstrate how their artistic values and practices were antithesis to the prevailing moral norms or dominant social practices, or to show how they radically deviated from them: rebellion was good in itself, and true art was nothing other than rebellion. All that Wim T. Schippers needed to do in order to be ranked among the avant-garde was empty a glass of water into the North Sea. Phil Bloom became a notorious rebel for reading the Christian newspaper *Trouw* naked on television, and Johnny van Doorn (a.k.a. Johnny the Selfkicker) became a public terror by rapping chaotic sentences devoid of any decipherable meaning at great speed.

I am not mentioning all these examples of artistic rebellion of the 1960s in order to dismiss them as futile or meaningless, but

to point out the fact that rebellion – and in a certain sense
engagement as well – needs no external motivation in order to
justify itself. In effect, it is or can be part of a particular attitude
or *ethos,* the ethos that the philosopher Michel Foucault once
described as the refusal to be ruled in any way whatsover. This
formulation comes close to existentialism, but it primarily ties
in with the famous maxim of Immanuel Kant, who defined the
Enlightenment as people's 'way out' from a condition of immaturity for which they themselves are responsible. Sartre's 'evil
eye' comes fairly close to Kant's self-imposed immaturity, which
can, of course, be explained by a love of ease and habituation:
it is so easy, so nice to let yourself be herded around and ruled
over. Kant also considered the Enlightenment to be a typical
individual act of resistance, but in a later text devoted to the
consequences of the French Revolution he also discussed the
collective dimensions of rebellion and revolt. In the early 1980s,
it was Foucault once again who established a link between the
two texts and thus imbued the term engagement with new life
20 years after the heyday of existentialism. According to
Foucault, Kant was implying that it was neither the revolution
itself nor the deeds and ideas of the revolutionaries that determined its importance or significance, but that the *enthusiasm*
of the more or less passive bystanders and spectators was
the most important indicator of the historic importance of the
revolution. That enthusiasm guarantees, in a certain sense,
that the revolution does not remain an isolated event, but is
connected with memories of earlier moments of resistance and
also points forward in time to new moments of rebellion and
resistance.

The enthusiasm of the bystanders offers us a completely
different perspective on engagement than is furnished by
existentialism, which usually presented it as an ultimately
unfounded and radically individual choice, as a kind of *creatio
ex nihilo*, a deed that ultimately does not seem to be much more
than a gesture. In Kant's example, engagement is a consequence
of a radical event, which sparks enthusiasm in many people and
is anything but something that originates from an autonomous
choice taken by an isolated individual. Nevertheless, it is only
possible if individuals are prepared to throw off their immaturity.
This account of the relationship between personal Enlightenment and enthusiasm for the revolution is eminently applicable
to the rebellious 1960s and offers the opportunity to inter the
unfounded and absurd radicalism of the existentialists in the
museum of ideological blunders. It is not the radical act of
resistance of the artist or intellectual that forms the kernel of

resistance, rebellion or civil disobedience, but the enthusiasm or the engagement of all those who do not themselves take part in the rebellion itself. Engagement is not an individual choice, but the expression of collective commitment to a crucial movement or development. This means that engagement is also not something that you can ascribe to separate, individual works of art or artistic achievements, but that it is always a collective affair. It is also not a one-off *decision* (something that you take or leave on rational or emotional grounds), but something that follows from a more or less long-standing or intensive commitment to something that transcends the individual. Engagement is nothing more than the intensification of a commitment which was always present, but which often remained unconscious. It is not an individual choice or decision: by definition, engagement precedes the individual. Engagement is not the decision that a beach lies hidden beneath the asphalt, but the *discovery* that such a thing is among the possibilities. That discovery might be an artistic or intellectual act, and as such will be ascribed to some individual or another, but as an event it is a collective affair.

3   Artist and public: the problem of the collective
We have gone beyond the individual, but we are far from having the slightest notion of what it means to form a collective: you could call this the contemporary cultural condition, and thus the ultimate artistic and intellectual challenge. *We have gone beyond the individual*: here I want to indicate that the individual is no longer a problem, an issue or a *casus belli*. The individual has been emancipated, has thrown off the oppressive shackles of feudality, tradition, stifling social control and religion, and now stands to some extent on his or her own two feet. That is the net result of two centuries of civic emancipation. We must be careful here, since we are primarily referring to 'the West'. Fouad Laroui is a novelist of Moroccan origin who writes in French and lives in the Netherlands. He, like no other writer, verbalizes and portrays the problems faced by all those migrants in his novels. These people wrestle in-between Western and non-Western culture, faced with the cultural task of becoming an individual as well as being subject to the equally self-evident cultural pressure to continue being part of a collective tradition which has little, if anything, to do with that same Western culture. The dilemmas in Laroui's novels make it clear that we had better leave behind the age-old conflict between tradition and modernity, the age-old conflict between the value of the collective, the security and manageability, but also the arbitrariness

of the small-scale, closed *community* on the one hand, and the value of the openness and freedom of modern *society*, which is vested only on the initiatives and the inventiveness of the individuals who actually make that society possible, on the other. This old conflict is based on a double error: on the nostalgic glorification of the solidarity and coherence of the traditional community and on the overly naive and optimistic projections of a heroic individual who would 'briefly' break away from that community. We are now confronted with the issue of how we can embed that errant individual (we ourselves, we the public) in a new collective, in a context within which each of us can say: yes, that is me, and yes, I belong there.

In the rebellion of the 1960s, the response to the question of where we belonged was usually rather unambiguous. We were 'children of the future', to quote the rock singer Steve Miller, and the key to that future was first and foremost the classic ideals of the Enlightenment – liberation, emancipation, democratization – even though a fairly broad spectrum of interpretations was used to flesh them out. The hippies especially went in for small-scale, quasi-agricultural communities in the bosom of 'nature', where free love, shared ideals and 'gettin' higher and higher' were the priority, while a diversity of other rebels opted for more political agendas which took socialism, democracy, sexual liberation, feminism and decolonization as their principal ingredients. Artists and intellectuals primarily played a role in the imagining of that future, in the evocation and representation of new, free forms of community, which in practice boiled down to either Rousseauian, nostalgic depictions of 'natural' forms, or small-scale community ('Born to be wild', you know), or to an endless rehashing of the many 20th-century variants of socialism, the abolition of private property, the introduction of forms of worker self-management and of local democratization. In short, the dream of a humanly engineered society, a *makeable* society, was left untouched, and the ideal of *collective* realization of such dreams was for many people still self-evident. It is strange, but it sometimes seems as if the representation of that collective makeability is interlinked with the universe and the era of black-and-white film (and television), which sacrificed those colourful details and nuances to the strict sobriety and the purifying, abstractive focus of a camera that wants to record that massiveness, anonymity, the large-scale and collectivity. The colour that was in fact added to the gaze of the media (film, photography, television) in the 1960s led to a radical individualization of that same gaze and perspective, and thus to an individualization of the many ideals and representations of a future societal form, and eventually to an undermining of those same ideals and images. *Makeability* has since been transformed from a collective and political project into an individual and cultural project. It has shifted from the government to the market, from the ideal of the welfare state to the ideal of the perfect, eternally young and healthy body, of the self-aware, flexible and independent individual. However, it is this very point that has raised the biggest doubts in recent years: the absolutization of the autonomy, the make-ability and the freedom of choice of that supremely celebrated and apparently untouchable and unmissable individual is being criticized and questioned from various angles. And when there is a hint of a revival of *engagement* or political, social or ideological commitment in the arts, then that can only be in relation to a deepening suspicion of the value and the role of that (post-) modern, liberal individual who procures his own oh so independent lifestyle at the furniture mall, the ethnic market in Beverwijk or at IKEA.

The problem of *engagement* in the arts is as big as the problem of the place of the individual in or in relation to a collective, whether an existing community or a collaborative project. There is good reason for the protests of foreign writers or actors against the automatism with which identifies them as *non-native* artists. This seems to reduce them to being interpreters or representatives of a specific *community*, while they at most interpret experiences that are, inter alia, lived by and from within that community – which certainly does not exclude them being able to represent or interpret completely different experiences as well. It is even worse when artistic expressions and products are read as *anticipations* of a future community, as harbingers of multicultural happiness or the absolute emancipation of every imaginable lifestyle or construable identity. Here we come close to traditional social realism, to Proletkult, to militant culture and worse things still, for example the exploitation of art as propaganda for any collective political project whatsoever. Yet the potential *engagement* of the arts and artists, as well as of intellectuals in a more general sense, depends – from the moment we extricate it from the age-old existentialist paradigm from which the whole idea was born – on that very act of *setting the agenda*, on making it a point for discussion or for thematization (verbalizing, representing, approaching) of that hopelessly complex issue of *collectivity*, call it community, call it the surplus value of society, call it citizenship, call it shared responsibility for the fate of the collective. That *collective* agenda dropped *progress* as its mantra some time ago. Enlightenment, progress, emancipation, liberation: these were the oft-repeated verbalizations of collective (and individual) projects which looked forward to a better future in the realization that, if we wanted, we could take that future into our own hands. We have especially attempted this using science, which formed the basis for permanent technological progress, and with politics, which was the source for a 'never-ending tour' of democratization and emancipation. Well then, that tour is now truly at an end. Science and politics are no longer regarded as important instruments that we can employ for the sake of emancipation, liberation or democratization that reaches further. A fundamental belief or trust in more far-reaching emancipation or democratization is practically nowhere to be found anyhow. Engagement (i.e. trust in and commitment to collective societal projects) has taken on a more defensive form. Faith in the future has stepped aside for scepticism as the fundamental attitude of an engaged lifestyle or cultural practice. The remarkable thing is that at the very moment we started to ask questions about faith in progress, universalism and the collective dreams of modern science and politics, the trust in *individuality* also – or for that very reason – seems to have taken a hefty knock. Perhaps this is paradoxical, but anyone who persists in going one single step further would ascertain that the rock-solid faith in the individual is nothing more than the net result of the combined effort of science and politics. We are *individual* because the sciences and (liberal) politics have *described* us as such, or rather, have *subscribed* to the existing 'societal' order, which thanks to this 'subscription' has been able to increasingly assume the form of a *marketplace*. In effect, our engagement begins at the market (not what the members of the old avant-garde and champions of pure art had ever intended), yet it cannot be squared with the activities that are generated on and through the marketplace, where all activity acknowledges only two identities: the individual as client and the mass as public (i.e. potential clients). Another relationship between the individual and the collective is unthinkable in the marketplace, yet is of vital importance when we begin to devote even a hint of a thought to notions like community, collectivity, neighbourhood, yes … even society. Over the last two decades, these notions have consistently been sacrificed to the brutal logic of the market, to the logic of 'global finance capital' and economic and cultural globalization, which has certainly broadened our cultural horizons but has also placed great strain on local, regional and national achievements, peculiarities and lifestyles.

The great cultural-political struggle of the coming decades will doubtless address the question of how we 'belong', what our collective identity, our status as a citizen of a nation state and as a member of the international community actually entails.

We have gone beyond progress. For most of us, progress, emancipation and individualization are behind us, like a realized project towering high. The future is not down to engagement (individual or otherwise), but depends on the (possibility of) community, of possible new collective correlations of meaning, lifestyles and forms of cooperation. Over the coming years, engagement in the artistic sense will be about the limitations and problems of makeability, in both the collective and the individual sense. It will bid farewell to every thought of progress and head off in search of an acceptable hedonism, in which the desire for and right to everyday and contemporary happiness is key, but without it also implying the sacrifice of the collective future to the individual's package of demands.

Do we just keep complaining about injustice, or do we set an example?

Hans Aarsman

In 1990, just after Saddam Hussein had invaded Kuwait, a story did the rounds that Iraqi troops had forced their way into the maternity ward of a Kuwaiti hospital. They had smashed the incubators and hurled the premature babies against the walls. The whole world was horrified, and me too. Get the Iraqis out of there, I thought, in chorus with plenty of other people. Now, more than a decade later, the story about splattered premature babies turns out to have been an American propaganda lie. Later, when the Americans had already left Iraq, Saddam Hussein ordered his troops to carry out a poison gas attack on a Kurdish village. The report might have been based on the truth, but it could just as easily have been the start of another American propaganda offensive. To this day, no poison gases have been discovered in Iraq. Did Saddam have them destroyed in time, or did he simply never have them? I will never forget the images of the corpses strewn across the road as recorded by the film camera that swept through the streets of the gassed village. Were they really dead, or were they acting? These are questions that I now ponder. It is even possible that the Kurds gassed their own people, in order to spur the international community to take action against Saddam. Something similar had already been tried in Bosnia.

You read the newspapers, you follow the television news, you brood and gossip in order to arrive at a balanced judgement. But what is it based on? There are so many things that you simply do not know, and what you do know cannot be trusted. You cannot trust photographs or film footage, and stories are completely untrustworthy. You are the plaything of those who transmit the facts, the media, even if the stories are harmless and devoid of propagandistic motives. After all, stories with a tragic undertone make a bigger impression than stories about happiness. That is why the greater part of what we get to see and hear is about social injustice. Sometimes there is one line reserved for good news – the closing phrase: '… and they lived happily ever after.' But the tragedy preceding it is the crux of the story.

In the 1980s I worked as a photographer for the *Nieuwe Revu* weekly newsmagazine. There I had a colleague, Kees Fontein, who had captured so many injustices on film that he wanted to show the other side of the coin for once, so off he went in search of happiness. *Nieuwe Revu* gave him three months to find it. He didn't get much further than the cliché of a couple of lovebirds in the park. Later it turned out to have been a businessman with his secretary. After publication, his wife discovered that he had been unfaithful … and left him. The businessman then sued *Nieuwe Revu* for damages, and the courts awarded the businessman compensation.

We haven't got the faintest notion of what happiness actually is.

A couple of years ago a group of black photographers from South Africa came to Amsterdam as part of an exchange programme. They had to take part in the obligatory symposium. We sat among the public, the five of them sitting behind a little table. I stuck my hand in the air. What did they think of Amsterdam? I asked. Beautiful city, they said. Were there things that they had photographed? They had seen absolutely nothing, they said. They had been walking around for two days, but their cameras had stayed in their bags, though they had wanted to take photos in the red light district; they thought that prostitutes displaying their wares behind glazed windows and junkies in alleyways were worth a photo, but their escort advised against it.

What about those bog-standard streets, where the average Amsterdammer spends his or her life? Had they seen any shots worth taking there? No, there was nothing of interest for them there.

Isn't that strange?

The people who live in such streets have a roof over their heads, they have food, and they will not be shot at. A street like that must seem like paradise to a South African from a township. Perhaps they don't have the visual apparatus to photograph happiness. Ultimately, they had come from a completely different environment. Then what if you grew up in such a street, like the majority of Dutch photographers? You might expect that they have no problem whatsoever with taking photos of such a street. Nevertheless, I have never seen a photo of a newly built neighbourhood in the Netherlands that brought a smile to my lips; or if it did, it was tongue in cheek.

Plenty of critical people on this planet feel concerned about the lot of humanity. They write, photograph, film, create art, pursue politics. They follow social developments, intercede for the oppressed, call for boycotts, create politically engaged work.

They throw themselves so passionately at the injustice in the
world that they don't see the other side of the coin, that of happiness. Whether due to a lack of fantasy, or a lack of guts, there
is in any case no critical, socially aware vision of happiness.
The result is that the impression of what happiness should be
is in the hands of commercial advertisers. They have every
opportunity to propagate the ideal that yields them the greatest
financial profit: an existence about power, status, luxury and
possessions. I cannot really empathize, but it seems that people
who lead an average, modal life like to mirror their lives on the
lives of eccentrics, the wealthy, the stars. In advertising jargon
they call it the consumer's 'aspiration level': the degree to
which the little man tries to emulate the rich. The odd individual
manages, at the expense of a whole mass of other people, to
get his hands on the pot of gold, while the rest simply miss the
boat and are stuck sitting sour-faced in front of the television.
Such a world full of avarice, split into winners and losers, is
begging to harbour injustice, which the critics can then passionately denounce. In consequence, a number of pennies are
occasionally tranferred into someone else's hands, but nothing
fundamentally changes. The only way to implement change is
if we can achieve a non-commercial realization of happiness.

Sometimes I come across a little saying:
'Success is getting what you want; happiness is wanting what
you get.'
That's putting it a bit too mildly. Surely happiness cannot be
about uncritically accepting everything that happens to you?
Sometimes I come across a book.
The English photographer Julian Germain showed me the proofs
of a book about an elderly gentleman from a typical English
working-class neighbourhood. One day Germain was walking
along a street full of drab terraced houses with his camera
bag. One of the houses caught his eye.

'It was yellow and orange. Actually it was a kind of shop. In the
large front bay window there were a few plants on sale for
unusual prices; for example 57p or 34p or 83p. I went inside and
there I found a few more plants. The bottom half of the walls was
wood panelled and painted bright yellow; above that they were
decorated, probably in the 1970s, with a floral style wallpaper.
Charlie Snelling appeared; quietly spoken, elderly, polite. He
told me what the various flora were and said that yes, he would
be happy to put some to one side for me until later. We talked
for a while and then I asked if he would mind looking after my

camera tripod, since I had decided I wouldn't be using it the rest of the day.

He took me through to his living room and showed me where he would put it, 'just to be safe'. On the walls of this equally brightly decorated room there were numerous photographs of a lady I immediately understood was his wife. I said I thought they were lovely pictures and he told me that Betty had died, a few years ago now.'

When Germain returned later that same day for the plants and the tripod, Charlie presented him with a sandwich and a cup of tea. He brought out a photo album with even more photos of his wife. When they had finished looking through them, Germain asked whether he might take some photos of Charlie. That was fine. A week later, Germain sent one of the prints with the request if he might come around again. That is how their friend-ship started – tea, a sandwich and some biscuits.

'Charlie was a simple, gentle man. He loved flowers and the names of flowers. He loved colour and surrounded himself with colour. He loved his wife. He was totally unambitious, all he wanted was for his children to be happy. Occasionally he would ask if I'd like to listen to some music and then he might play, for example, just three songs from a Nat King Cole LP, but we would really listen to them. Without ever trying or intending to, he showed me that the most important things in life cost nothing at all. He was my antidote to modern living.'

Charlie Snelling passed on in 2000.

Germain compiled the book *For every minute you are angry you lose sixty seconds of happiness* from pages in Charlie's family album and from photos that he had taken of him. It is a template model for what critical engagement should strive to achieve in our day and age: forget the 'winners' and the 'losers' and provide examples of people who operate in a different forcefield. People who are not grasping, not filled with self-importance and not embittered, people with a profound under-standing of who they are and what they stand for, something that cuts across all cultures.

We cannot personally invent life; we have to follow someone's example. There have been times when local tradition provided the examples; now the media have stepped into that role. Do not leave this important task to the commercially driven. Stand up for who you are, no matter what the adverts try to turn you into. Put forward examples of characters who lead lives that

are styleful and courageous, social but not submissive. People
who will not allow themselves to be pushed into the sidelines
because of set-backs, as they accept that adversity is an inex-
tricable aspect of life. In a world that holds such examples
high, social injustice will disappear automatically.

Beyond postmodern melancholy
Critical pessimism versus 'glocal' panic –
the 'new commitment'

Lieven De Cauter

Those historic signals, collectively received and transmitted, which together make up the swarm of things that are 'up in the air' and determine the character and sensitivity of an era, we sometimes, for the most part unthinkingly, call the *Zeitgeist*, the spirit of the age. This spirit is dismissed by some, not wholly incorrectly, as a metaphysical ghost, a more common practical version of Hegel's *Weltgeist* (absolute spirit, *logos*, reason, God who would realize himself in the becoming of the world, as history). But the spirit of the age does exist, even if we refuse to believe in a world spirit as reasonable, or even refuse to use the expression at all. It is impossible to deny that the character, the 'temperature' of an age can change intangibly but quite unmistakably and certainly faster and more fundamentally than we, on our daily treadmill, will realize or want to admit. The world changes too fast for us to be able to record, without threatening the continuity of everyday life.

The 1960s were a time of revolt, involvement, hope, emancipation, participation, experimentation and often farcical reversals. These were the years which marked the rise of the informal society. The crisis of the 1970s, mainly due to troubles with oil, brought about a *retour à l'ordre*, which people were quick to call postmodernism: the end of the great narratives (Jean-François Lyotard), exhaustion of the supply of utopian energy (Jürgen Habermas), obsolescence of 'the new' as a category (Gianni Vattimo). Lyotard speaks of 'une sorte de chagrin dans le Zeitgeist', a kind of chagrin, wistfulness, melancholy or grief embodied in the spirit of the age. 'Social criticism' and 'involvement' seemed definitely to belong to the past (even the words have sounded stale for years). The 1980s saw the triumph of neo-liberalism (remember Thatcher and Reagan) and the flowering of the yuppie consumption culture. In the mid-1980s the transition from the industrial to the post-industrial society became an accomplished fact and the free market was elevated to the status of a theological dogma (with a Holy Trinity comprising privatization, liberalization and deregulation). The word capitalism was hardly ever used because capitalism was so omnipresent, like water to a fish. The fall of the Berlin Wall in 1989 seemed to prove that capitalism was the inevitable outcome of history, and so to be accepted as both 'natural' and 'necessary'. The euphemisms of the marketeers swept across the world. Injustice vanished behind facile catchwords like 'delocalization', 'transnational strategies', 'corporate identity', 'human resource management', sexy terms like 'upscaling' and 'downscaling', the culture of the logo and the house style: image was everything. The 1990s saw the definitive breakthrough of the new Network Society, characterized by information technology and globalisation. There seemed to be no room left for criticism. 'Keep up with the acceleration' was the message. Sensitivity for trends was the only guide.

Until suddenly, as if from nowhere, a bolt from the blue sky of carefree neo-capitalism, came mass protest, world-wide, bearing names like Seattle, Genoa and Porto Allegre. The wave of protest that raised its head in 1998 was imme-diately named a political movement: anti-globalism, forcefully amended by its supporters into 'other globalism'. Thanks to this movement social criticism and involvement were back on the agenda. Suddenly thousands of people, even hundreds of thousands, were convinced that the new neo-liberal world order which was in the process of establishing itself all over the world was profoundly wrong, and wrong in every possible way: economically, socially, in humanitarian respect, culturally and ecologically.

It appeared that the realization that this world order was neither 'natural' nor 'necessary' was beginning to dawn on many people, many of whom would not dream of describing themselves as alternative globalists. This was the realization that marked the beginning of the twenty-first century: a feeling, a growing understanding, that our world is untenable. Its fail-ings are legion. Injustice, exploitation and planetary exhaustion can only lead to a series of catastrophes. The twenty-first century announces itself a century of permanent catastrophe. We are enmeshed in total mobilization, an acceleration which expresses itself in swelling streams of information, mobility, migration, ecological disasters, ozone warnings, heat waves and the rest. Total mobilization, resulting from modernization, from progress, comes in a phase of turbulence and catastrophe. Moreover, ecological disaster (global warming) and the con-tinuing demographic explosion (by 2050 we will have been joined by a further three billion people), will pave the way to mass migration from the south and east. What now?

The architect, and more particularly the urbanist, finds himself at the centre of all this commotion. 'Sprawl', the dis-ruption of town and countryside, is his field of activity. The mega-cities of the twenty-first century could well become eco-logical and humanitarian disaster areas. Can 'the ideology of urbanism' go on being what Rem Koolhaas in 1995 was still defining polemically as 'accepting what exists'?

Marx, in his widely known eleventh proposition on Feuer-bach, wrote that what the world needed was not just inter-pretation, but change. It was no longer enough to philosophize about reality: philosophy needed to be made practical. Philos-ophy can only be sublimated by realizing it and only be realized by its sublimation (according to the phrasing in Marx ' critique of Hegel's philosophy of law). Adorno used the converse as the basic starting point of his negative dialectic: 'Philosophy, which at one time seemed to have been outdated, lives on, because the opportunity to realize it has been missed'. According to him it cannot be given up without defeatism, 'after the attempts to change the world have failed'. The theme underlying Adorno's thinking was recent historical disillusionment: the Enlighten-ment, the avant-garde, the socialist revolutions, in short modernity, had not kept their promises and had in fact proved catastrophic. He called this the 'dialectic of enlightenment'.

Since the rise of the alternative globalization movement people have gone back to Esperanto in the vein of Marx: 'Un aultro mundo es possivel'. We no longer have a feeling of his-toric disillusionment (or have learnt to live with the fact that history is not a trip to the promised land, that Paradise is not just round the corner and that utopian expectations of paradise have their hellish side). But many people, faced by the facts, are no longer capable of anything but interrupting, at set times, the *vita contemplativa* of art, culture and academic life, the *scholè*, the spare time occupied in study, in favour of a *vita activa*. That, as I see it, is the historic context, the 'spirit of the age' within which the 'new commitment' is becoming under-standable.

A new optimism? I would rather call it critical pessimism. The new commitment derives not from utopian, messianic or Marxist expectations of eternal well-being, but from an aware-ness of urgency prompted by the string of catastrophes experienced under the gruesome constellation of the new imperial world order. In this world order America and its military-industrial complex rules the world through 'full spectrum dominance' and 'multiple simultaneous major theatre wars' and at the same time provokes, smokes out and ensures the continued existence of terrorism. Is this a kind of defeatism? In my view, critical pessimism is not defeatism. Critical pes-simism[1] is the converse of uncritical optimism, and uncritical

optimism is second nature to the political classes and captains
of industry.

Until now commitment has been supported by deep,
utopian or idealistic (or even religious, messianic) optimism,
but today, more than ever, it is coming to be time to accept
pessimism, more specifically critical or self-critical pessimism,
as the motto, motif and motor for a planetary protest. On Sunday
15 February 2003 something like 10 million people took to the
streets in protest against the war in Iraq. This was new in the
history of mankind: never before had so many people taken to
the streets on a single day. Statistically the number should be
increased (because the old, the sick, the shy and the lazy stayed
away, as did those who were prevented by work or special
circumstances), so one could conclude that a significant portion
of mankind said a unquestionable no to the war. Was this the
beginning of a planetary mobilization (or anti-mobilization
movement) against the New Imperial World order, against
'glocal' panic (an instinctive local reaction to global developments), against a capsular civilization and against ecological
mutilation of the planet?

But are these forces that still can be countered, are we
not already – against our better judgement, willingly or unwill-
ingly and only because we are living at this time at this spot on
the earth – involved and implicated in or accessory to universal
processes, unstoppable and uncontrollable. For example,
record temperatures are being experienced as I write, the
hottest days since meteorological measurements began are
being recorded all over Europe. If, sometime soon, we all have
air conditioning, the resulting pollution will raise temperatures
even further, which means we will have to buy more air conditioning, which will produce still more pollution, and so on.
'Commitment' would seem to offer no hope in the face this
kind of chain reaction, hopelessly naive in the face of the thousands of such feedback mechanisms which together make up
'the state of the planet'. But just because of that it is impossible
to doubt that there is some reason for Commitment. It's Red
Alert on Planet Earth. Time to take action. But how?

The converse of critical pessimism is glocal panic. 'Leef-
baar Rotterdam' [Liveable Rotterdam] and the Pim Fortuyn
phenomenon were clear examples of glocal panic. Just like Le
Pen in France and the Flemish Block votes in Flanders must be
seen this way: demographics and migration are changing our
world so rapidly that people are developing defensive reactions
and adopting solutions which are both simplistic and reactionary. Glocal panic is one of the most dangerous reactions of

the age and is having more and more effect on politics. The best, perhaps the only way to counter glocal panic, seems to be to look at things globally: to understand globalization and interpret local processes in the light of globalization (precisely what our media-dominated politics, complying to compulsive, soap opera-like proximity omits to do).

Critical pessimism teaches us how to deal with paradoxes, even its own paradoxes. Even commitment is paradoxical. In the spring of 1981, in a moment of profane enlightenment, I wrote, in an overstretched synthesis of Nietzsche, Marx, Adorno and Benjamin, what has since become one of my fundamental maxims: ' The world can not be improved without abolishing it, but improving the world means to go against its abolition'. Like Nietzsche I believed that all religion, all idealism, is bent on negating or even abolishing, as it were, the world as it is, in favour of a superior, later, different world, a world beyond, a *Hinterwelt*, and that it is the task of the philosopher to oppose this abolition or negation. Like Marx I believed that it was not enough simply to interpret the world, but I did not believe that mankind could be changed without being abolishing it (as every totalitarian system has shown). Like Adorno and Benjamin I believed that progress and enlightenment, particularly in their technological and economic logic of growth, have in them a catastrophic logic which must be combated in the interests of the planet – and in this context, the report of the Club of Rome was surely an important beacon – and so on. In short, I found that this paradoxical formula gave a good indication of the impossible but necessary position of criticism (commitment, protest and resistance) at the end of the twentieth century, in a *fin de siècle* spirit of the age, a premature and protracted ending to the millennium. But I could not have suspected that a good twenty years later that last – combating the abolition of the world – would need to be taken so literally.

Perhaps even this new commitment is no more than a trend, a transient phenomenon (perhaps to be blamed on the wave of self-confidence generated by the economic boom of the 1990s) and ultimately we will all submit ourselves meekly to the New Imperial World order, or give way to the defence mechanisms and flight reactions of glocal panic. During the Iraq war (which is still not officially over) expressions of protest in America were censored by a wave of patriotism and where if necessary punished by dismissal. Protests in France, Germany and Belgium were received with threats and reprisals. In Spain there was even a suggestion of a bill to imprison people who protested against a war. All these were signs of the time. The spirit of the age of the 'new commitment' will probably shatter against the walls of the New Imperial World order. And the rise of a 'capsular civilization' will necessarily turn us all into frightened creatures, all in different ways seized by forms of glocal panic. That is my pessimism. But it is precisely this image of doom (which, sadly enough, becomes more real every day) that proves the necessity of commitment, with or against whatever the spirit of the age may be. Another world is not only possible, it is in the first place necessary.

Note

1   Term (attributed to Pieter Uyttenhove) launched in the context of the debates in Studio Open City, a mainly Belgian network of architecture teachers, taken up enthusiastically by the student and architectural journal *De loeiende koe*. As my position fitted the description, I adapted the term as my own.

Intervention in the relations of production, or sublimation of contradictions?

On commitment then and now

The intellectual positions of Walter Benjamin and Theodor Adorno have lost none of their relevance as benchmarks in the debate on commitment. They can be seen as two points of view that mark the limits of the field within which the game of commitment can be played. Benjamin and Adorno were both left-wing philosophers with a thorough knowledge of Marxism who developed variants of their own. Each of them advocated in his own way a committed art, but the direct consequences of their standpoints for artistic practice are very different. (The texts to which I refer were written as reflections on literature, but mutatis mutandis they can also be applied to other artistic forms.)

Benjamin's most radical text on commitment is 'The author as producer', a lecture given in Paris in 1934 at the Moscow-sponsored 'Congress of anti-fascist writers in the defence of culture'. In this text Benjamin defends the thesis that there is a direct connection between the literary technique of a work, its political tendency (reactionary or progressive), and the place of the author in the process of production. Benjamin claims that the work of many 'left-wing' authors has not had any revolutionary impact, but has been fully assimilated within the bourgeois pattern of expectation: 'For we are faced with the fact (...) that the bourgeois apparatus of production and publication can assimilate astonishing quantities of revolutionary themes, indeed, can propagate them without calling its own existence, and the existence of the class that owns it, into question.'[1]

For Benjamin this means that it is not enough for the content of a text to manifest commitment. Genuinely progressive authors must propagate the revolution not only by what they write, but also by opting for a different position in the process of production. Instead of satisfying the bourgeois pattern of expectations and making use of existing publication outlets, they must develop alternative procedures in which they bridge the gap between 'readers' and 'writers' as much as possible. That process was under way in the Soviet Union, he claimed, where posters and interactive media turned as many people as possible into writers, and it should be followed elsewhere.

Adorno's most accessible piece on commitment is a lecture from 1962. Adorno is on his guard, even more than Benjamin, and for other reasons, against writers who are only too blatantly 'committed'. Committed art that sets out to convince the public of a particular point of view by aesthetic means is based, Adorno argues, on false premises. After all, in so far as it is art, it is subject to the autonomous formal laws of the medium within which it works. In that constellation, the intention of the artist is merely one moment in the whole process, and that moment cannot be the sole determinant of the final result. A work of art like Picasso's *Guernica* is in the first place an autonomous work of art: it was not created with the primary and only intention of exposing the crimes of the German occupying forces. Nevertheless, it does that precisely because, as a work of art, it is a critical reflection on the given reality. 'Even autonomous works of art like the *Guernica* are determinate negations of empirical reality: they destroy what destroys, what merely exists and as mere existence recapitulates the guilt endlessly. (…) The artist's imagination is not a creatio ex nihilo; only dilettantes and sensitive types conceive it as such. By opposing empirical reality, works of art obey its forces, which repulse the spiritual construction, as it were, throwing it back upon itself.'[2]

It is in that complex relation with reality that the critical force of art lies – not in the deliberate commitment of the artist. Adorno even recognizes a manifest danger in the latter: 'Hidden in the notion of a "message", of art's manifesto, even if it is politically radical, is a moment of accommodation to the world: the gesture of addressing the listener contains a secret complicity with those being addressed, who can, however, be released from their illusions only if that complicity is rescinded.'[3]

The fact of wanting to communicate a message implies conformity to the norms of communicability and comprehensibility imposed by the socially dominant rational thought. This entails a betrayal of the specificity of art, which consists precisely of non-conformity and, through this act of resistance, offering a refuge to what is different. Only by remaining true to itself can art really criticise and keep alive the hope of something different.

It is not difficult to characterise the situation of architecture in the 1960s and 1970s in terms of these positions of Benjamin and Adorno. This is the period when CIAM thinking came to an end. The mobilizing power of modernist discourse had ebbed away, and the modal practice of modern architecture coincided to a large extent with the mainstream building programmes that turned the historic cities thoroughly upside-down and were further primarily responsible for depressing urban expansions. Two contradictory tendencies emerged as a critical reaction to this discouraging state of affairs, even though they both embodied a specific form of commitment: the populist participation movement, on the one hand; and the visionary architecture of Constant, Utopie, Superstudio and so on, on the other.

The participation movement implemented Benjamin's position. For example, Giancarlo De Carlo's 1972 call 'For a justification of architecture' led to the thesis that it is the task of the architect to discover the genuine needs of the users and to help them to express themselves. The aim was 'creative participation', as a result of which the social order would be disrupted by disorderly, revolutionary impulses. To achieve this objective, however, architects had to understand their own role in a new way. As Benjamin posits that the progressiveness of a literary product depends on the role of the author in the process of production, so De Carlo made the change in the role of the architect a condition of social change.[4] The analysis of the populists alleged that the modernist architects used their specialist knowledge as an instrument of power to impose bourgeois norms and values on the users. Even when these architects explicitly aimed at improving the living conditions of the working class, they did so in a way that deprived the workers of a voice and alienated them from their own environment. That was why the process of production must be altered in such a way that architects were no longer the only ones to make decisions, but that residents and users could have a clear impact on the design.[5]

The other extreme was represented by a number of architects and would-be architects who operated in the border zone between architecture and art: Yona Friedman and GEAM, Hans Hollein and Walter Pichler, Haus-Rucker-Co, Constant, the French group Utopie, Superstudio, and Archizoom. Their projects consisted of visionary schemes and constructions that were presented with varying degrees of aplomb as utopian futures. They can be regarded as idiosyncratic products of an architectural practice that gives priority to its own autonomy as a visual idiom and wants to issue a critique of the state of affairs in society from that autonomous position. Constant, for example, situated his project *New Babylon* explicitly within a (Neo-)Marxist critique of society and presented his vision of the future as the 'antithesis to the lie society' based on a completely new division of the means of production.[6] The work of Superstudio was also presented as a form of critique of society.[7] But what these projects have in common is the fact that they did not aim at any direct application of their commitment, but translated this commitment in a very indirect way into images that then acquired the status of, say, a 'negative Utopia'. (A negative Utopia shows the ultimate consequences of taking existing social tendencies to their limit. That terrifying picture is supposed to lead to an awareness of the urgent necessity to resist the status quo. In other words, there is only hope in the horror – 'il n'y a de l'espoir que dans l'horreur'.)[8]

Both tendencies came to an end in the course of the 1970s. The participation movement faded out, among other reasons because the experiences with participation did not bring about the hoped-for renewal, but on the contrary often led to an insipid and aesthetically very disappointing result. Only those architects who sublimated the contribution of residents and users in a design that went beyond faithful obedience to their demands managed to produce significant complexes.[9] Usually, however, the participation process resulted in a lifeless and literal translation of the uninspiring demands of the users. What is more, the mechanisms of participation did not always reach the targeted 'base' because in the first place the most outspoken individuals raised their voices while those most in need were neglected. Although a few die-hards continued to believe in the participation model (Lucien Kroll, for example), the vast majority of architects have abandoned it. In many countries the specific achievements of the campaign for participation are taken for granted by now – the publishing of plans, public inquiries, hearings, and so on – but the 'battle for the city' no longer hits the headlines of the architecture journals.

As for the visionary architecture, in the last resort it never managed to escape from the effect about which Benjamin had already warned: it became fully assimilated in the circuit of publications, galleries and museums that gave the provocatively intended collages and scale models the innocent status of works of art. The most vehement critique of the position of visionary architecture has been formulated by Manfredo Tafuri. According to Tafuri, it was a historical mistake for the visionary architects to avoid direct involvement in the mass production of buildings. In doing so they were satisfied with an extremely peripheral position from where all they could do was to make marginal comments. Their work thus rendered itself powerless and inefficient: 'It is hardly worth mentioning here that, in a capitalistic system, there is no break between production, distribution and consumption. All the intellectual anti-consumer Utopias that seek to redress the ethical "distortions" of the technological world by modifying the system of production or the channels of distribution only reveal the complete inadequacy of their theories, in the face of the actual structure of the capital economic cycle.'[10]

Seen in structural terms, the *Exodus* project of Rem Koolhaas, Elia Zenghelis, Madelon Vriesendorp and Zoe Zenghelis (1972) can be seen as both the culmination and the end of the road of the visionary architecture of the 1960s. *Exodus or the Voluntary Prisoners of Architecture*, as the full title runs, is a design for the creation of a linear zone to run right through the centre of London, 'protected' from the rest of the city by two parallel walls. Between these walls a sequence of rectangles, all of the same size, is situated, within which constantly changing scenarios take place. The scenarios describe a variety of programmes, varying from ceremonial spaces and temporary housing to baths and museums, each in an idiosyncratic architectural style of its own that turns the conventional patterns of expectation upside-down. The idea is that this strip should prove so attractive to Londoners that it would awaken them from their slumber and get them to experience the true intensity of the metropolitan ideal. It would tempt them to escape from London to the new enclave. This impulsive exodus would turn them into the voluntary prisoners of the strip.[11] This design contains echoes of Rem Koolhaas' experiences in Berlin during a study excursion in 1971: 'That year the wall celebrates its tenth birthday. My first impression in the hot August weather: the city seems almost completely abandoned, as empty as I always imagined the other side to be. Other shock: it is not East Berlin that is imprisoned, but the West, the "open society". In my imagination, stupidly, the wall was a simple, majestic north-south divide; a clean, philosophical demarcation; a neat, modern Wailing Wall. I now realize that it encircles the city, paradoxically making it "free".'[12]

Exodus, like the Berlin Wall, illustrates the potential and ambiguities of architecture. The utopian belief in the possibility of moulding society by architecture is confirmed and denied by it at the same time – confirmed in that a structure that is in principle simple acquires an enormous impact through political decisions that can mean life or death to anyone who wants to climb over the wall; denied in that the Berlin Wall is never regarded as 'architecture' in the traditional sense of the word (as a construction built with deliberately aesthetic intentions, with a certain symbolic significance, and a well-considered architectural style). On the basis of the Berlin experiences with the ambiguous power of architecture, *Exodus* presents itself as an anti-utopian project. It is a manifesto about the essential ambivalence of architecture, which both seduces and oppresses, which can equally stand for liberation or terror.

This complex position, which was later developed by Koolhaas in his *Delirious New York* and *S, M, L, XL*, and by OMA in its architectural projects, is hard to reconcile with the term 'commitment'. Commitment, after all, presupposes that a definite choice is made for or against certain things. A committed position does not readily allow space for ambiguity and ambivalence. Koolhaas himself will therefore use the word sparingly, but at most speak of a 'critical' attitude. His well-known metaphor of the surfer on the waves does not immediately evoke the picture of a committed intellectual either, but rather of an impassioned aesthete who makes use of every opportunity to fulfil his passion.

In this sense Koolhaas' trajectory fits in with the development of the 'narcissistic stage' that Alexander Tzonis and Liane Lefaivre have detected in the architecture of the late 1970s. They characterize this stage by: '1) *formalism*, a marked preoccupation with the purely visual features of architectural designs, 2) *graphism*, a fascination with the evocative power of drawings and models, 3) *hedonism*, a tendency to view design only as a source of gratification, 4) *élitism*, the conviction that the architect is the supreme judge of the quality of the built environment, 5) *avant-gardism*, a strong belief in the uniqueness and originality of their own ideas, and 6) *anti-functionalism*, the rejection not only of the functionalist aesthetic, but the very idea of function itself.'[13]

This somewhat exaggerated description applied in the first place to the architecture of the New York five and the Italian Neo-Rationalists, but it can also be applied to the vast majority of the architects whom Heinrich Klotz classified under the heading 'Revision der Moderne'.[14] The ambitious exhibition of the same name organised in the Deutsches Architektur Museum in Frankfurt showed work by Mario Botta, Peter Eisenman, Frank Gehry, Maurizio Grassi, Michael Graves, Hans Hollein, Rob Krier and Aldo Rossi, but also by Superstudio, OMA and others. The highly divergent formal idioms developed in these oeuvres, varying from a flamboyant revival of a classicistic idiom and a distillation of a traditional urban architecture to a reinterpretation of constructivism, did not prevent observers from regarding the farewell to commitment as almost the most decisive characteristic of this generation. The modernist project was considered to have failed – the attempt to change the world by architecture had apparently been based on a mistaken premise – and that was why architects were returning in droves to 'l'architecture pour l'architecture'.

Of course, there were critics who regretted this turn of events. Michael Müller, for instance, soon argued that this preoccupation with the 'outward appearance' of architecture marked a regression to a nineteenth-century position in which the social role of architecture that the modernists had put on the agenda was simply denied.[15] And Kenneth Frampton's 'critical regionalism' was an attempt to pick out the best parts of postmodernism by focusing attention on a number of architectural practices that he still considered to have social relevance.[16] Another strategy aimed to deploy the Adornian interpretation of the autonomy of art to legitimise architecture for architecture's sake. An example of this can be found in an article of 1981 by Geert Bekaert, in which he argued, referring to Tafuri, that architecture was caught up in an impasse: either it surrenders to the direct dictation of the social forces that follow the laws of the logic of consumption, or it turns its back on them and appropriates an autonomous domain that is nevertheless doomed to remain socially ineffectual or to be recuperated within the very logic of consumption against which it had rebelled. In his conclusion, that he considers to be no more than 'chasing a costly fantasy', Bekaert argues that the only way to escape from this impasse lies in architecture itself: fighting architecture with architecture, through the constant reintroduction of a poetic moment.[17]

These attempts to rescue commitment in architecture, however, were far from dominant in the architectural culture of the 1980s and 1990s. At a time when Neo-Liberalism dominated political thought, such summons were no more than scarcely audible calls from the wings. Architectural culture had massively turned its back on the 'utopian' intentions of modern architecture – by now it had almost become an insult to accuse an architect of producing 'utopian' designs – and it seemed to be a generally accepted fact that architecture could not resolve any social issues and should therefore not entertain any social ambitions. Architects retreated to their own terrain – the design of beautiful buildings – and left the rest up to sociologists and planners. The journals reported on fantastic buildings, new talents and new trends, and found a growing audience for it all. Architecture became trendy, part of a lifestyle consciousness, and thus more and more streamlined in order to meet the demands of a trendsetting class. Anyone who found fault with that was a groaner.

The people behind this book believe that the number of groaners has grown since, and the call for commitment is now being heard much more clearly. That is not surprising in itself. In the search for ever new themes and perspectives that are needed to keep the production of architectural publications going, it is not so strange that in the end we find ourselves with a theme that seems to have been out of sight for long enough for

it to be presented as something fresh and new today. Besides,
a number of social indicators have reached such an alarming
level (the twin attacks on the World Trade Center, the murder
of Dutch politician Pim Fortuyn) that perhaps the complacency
of the 1990s is running out at last. If that really is the case, it
seems to me to be a positive sign for the vitality and pertinence
of the architectural culture.

Okwui Enwezor organised 'Documenta 11' based on the
idea of a critical methodology of interdisciplinarity that is
appropriate to a global public sphere in which critical models
and ideas of artists and intellectuals can be presented and
discussed.[18] Such a critical methodology of interdisciplinarity
can also be beneficial for architecture. It is a good thing to open
up the closed domain of architecture again and to raise questions
that have for too long been regarded as marginal or irrelevant.
Themes such as mobility, sustainability or equality of opportunity are and remain of crucial importance for architecture.
However, if we are to learn anything from the history of the last
fifty years, it is that, no matter how important such themes may
be, they cannot and should not determine architecture. They
cannot take the place of actual architectural thinking, in other
words, of design. To avoid the traps that have meant the end of
the ideals of participation and visionary architecture, a sort of
hybridization between the two attitudes ought to take place,
which combines the honest and direct involvement with social
themes and an intense labour of design that manages to convert
these themes into intriguing spaces that leave a lasting
impression.

Notes

1   Walter Benjamin, 'The Author as Producer', in: Walter Benjamin,
    Reflections, Schocken, New York 1986, p. 229.
2   T.W. Adorno, 'Commitment', in: *Notes to Literature*, vol. 2, pp. 76-
    94, p. 89.
3   Idem, p. 93.
4   Giancarlo De Carlo, 'Voor een verantwoording van de archi-
    tectuur', *Forum*, XXIII (1972) no. 1, pp. 8-20.
5   See also Alexander Tzonis and Liane Lefaivre, 'In de naam van
    het volk', *Forum*, XXV (1976) no. 3, pp. 3-33.
6   See the chapter 'New Babylon: de antinomieën van de utopie', in:
    Hilde Heynen, *Architectuur en kritiek van de moderniteit*, SUN,
    Nijmegen 2001, pp. 212-239.
7   Cristiano Toraldo di Francia, 'Superstudio & Radicaux', in:
    Frédéric Migayrou (ed.), *Architecture radicale*, exh. cat. Institut
    d'Art Contemporain-IAC, Villeurbanne 2001, pp. 152-243.
8   Idem, p. 207.

9   See, among others, the comment by Manfredo Tafuri on Giancarlo
     De Carlo's project for Matteoti: Manfredo Tafuri, *History of Italian
     Architecture, 1944-1985*, MIT Press, Cambridge (Mass.) 1990, pp.
     119-121.
10   Manfredo Tafuri, 'Design and Technological Utopia', in: Emilio
     Ambasz, *Italy: The New Domestic Landscape. Achievements and
     Problems of Italian Design*, The Museum of Modern Art, New
     York 1972.
11   [OMA,] 'Exodus' (1972), *Architectural Design*, no. 5, 1977, pp.
     328-329. For an extensive analysis see: Lieven De Cauter and
     Hilde Heynen, 'De Exodusmachine', in: Otakar Mácel and Martin
     van Schaik (eds.), *Exit Utopia. Architectural Provocations
     1956–1976*, Prestel, Munich, in press.
12   Rem Koolhaas, 'field Trip', in: O.M.A., Rem Koolhaas and Bruce
     Mau, *S, M, L, XL*, 010 Publishers, Rotterdam 1995, pp. 212-233,
     pp. 216-219
13   Alex Tzonis and Liane Lefaivre, 'The Narcissist Phase in Archi-
     tecture', *Harvard Architecture Review*, vol. 1, Spring 1980, pp. 52-
     61, p. 54.
14   Heinrich Klotz (ed.), *Die Revision der Moderne. Postmoderne
     Architektur 1960–1980*, Prestel, Munich 1984.
15   Michael Müller, 'Over de "schone schijn" van de postmoderne
     architectuur', *Oase*, no. 13, 1986, pp. 2-16.
16   Kenneth Frampton, 'Towards a Critical Regionalism: Six Points
     for an Architecture of Resistance', in: Hal Foster (ed.), *The Anti-
     Aesthetic. Essays on Postmodern Culture*, Bay Press, Seattle
     1983, pp. 16-30.
17   Geert Bekaert, 'Het recht op architectuur', *Wonen-TA/BK*, no. 4,
     1981, pp. 9-17.
18   Okwui Enwezor, Adebayo Olukoshi and Heiko Sievers, 'Preface',
     in: Okwui Enwezor et al. (eds.), *Under Siege: Four African Cities
     Freetown, Johannesburg, Kinshasa, Lagos* (documenta 11_Plat-
     form 4), Hatje Cantz, Ostfildern-Ruit 2002.

The invisible in architecture

Ole Bouman

> Why have practical men not acquired credit? For the reason that architecture is born in discourse. Why not Men of Letters? For the reason that architecture is born of construction. To be an architect, one must seek discourse and construction together.
> Vitruvius

Architecture and engagement is a profoundly tedious subject. especially when it is presented as something new. Unless of course a new legitimacy were really to be advanced, a new mission for a discipline that has for years bemoaned its loss of social relevance and its marginalization on the building site. Yes, in that case there really would be something worth talking about. It would mean that a profession which can be regarded as the embodiment of fifty centuries of civilization could continue to shoulder that role. That someone capable of giving architecture a reason for existing for a further span of time had come along. Someone of the calibre of Vitruvius, Abbot Suger, Alberti, Palladio, Durand, Le Corbusier. See elsewhere in this book?

As yet, things look rather less threatening for the status quo. What, after all, is so new about all this? Architecture has always had a social task, hasn't it? No architect has ever been able to be 'disengaged', either in the distant past or more latterly, surely? In recent years, too, Dutch architects have been actively involved in major social projects like the Vinex urban expansion scheme, in 'mainports' and infrastructure, or in explicitly 'engaged' research projects like *Rotterdam 2045*. The present writer heads a magazine that has never, in all its 75-year history, stopped raising the issue of the social significance of architecture. But in this it is by no means unique. Day in, day out, there have always been some architects preoccupied with subjects that transcend their profession. On the other hand, it must also be said that among those presently flirting with engagement are many who only a little while ago firmly rejected any attempt to quiz them about the social motivation of their professional practice. Now that there has been a change in fashion, the motives are changing too. But whether that will also change the social significance of architecture is exceedingly doubtful.

As such, the question of architecture and engagement is as superfluous as it is inevitable. Superfluous because a professional discipline or an art that is so costly, that demands so much time of so many people in achieving its purpose, that is at the heart of society and visible to everyone, can never exist in and for itself alone. But inevitable, too, because no professional discipline or art form is so in need of an external justification, a reason, a motive, a task and a mission, as architecture. Architecture has never succeeded in emptying itself of functional significance. It *has* a programme and a debate about the nature of that programme is only to be expected.

But while these two variants of the same question belong together in the same way as the art of building and the craft of building, the remarkable thing about architecture is that the two appear to alternate in a historical succession, each in turn claiming hegemony in the debate on what architecture is really all about. And so, every now and then it becomes necessary to state the obvious, that architecture stands for something greater than itself. Only the next moment, I guarantee you now, having to stress once again that there is an autonomous moment in architecture that constitutes the discipline's core – a body of knowledge, something unique, a distinctive dynamic of action and reaction in an independent métier.

But not just yet. The issue now is how architecture, after years of postmodernist dis-engagement, of philosophical deconstruction and of digital experiments with form, can recover some measure of social significance. Become involved. Contribute something to the public cause. And even though there won't be any rush to establish a dogma for architecture as happened repeatedly in the past, there is nonetheless a strong need for a clearly defined task, a mandate that lends architecture its social relevance. In an overexposed culture in which it sometimes seems as if architecture has been reduced to the preserve of a very select group of celebrities who compete with one another for the few dozen prestigious projects that are available worldwide every year, there comes a moment when people want to return to the question of the invisible in architecture. The question of why.

The question of why is always of a different order from the questions of who, what and how. Anyone who is even moderately acquainted with architectural criticism and journalism knows that the last three questions are constantly being raised. There are newspapers and journals that concentrate on presenting new work (what). There are magazines devoted exclusively to the trials and tribulations of the superstars (who). And there are magazines about the methodical and technical elaboration of architecture (how). But there is no market for the why. Indeed, the question of why is always an implicit threat to the status quo and for that reason, in architecture as every-where else, it is raised as little as possible and then usually in passing. Those who persist in raising it can expect difficulties which is why the present popularity of the notion of engage-ment should be regarded with suspicion. Is it truly a token of doubt and reappraisal, and thus of risk, or is it simply another timely career-launching gimmick? Is it a form of sticking one's neck out, or a form of the right marketing technique at the right social moment?

The best test of whether engagement is about arriving at a better world, rather than enhancing individual status and market value, is the extent to which that engagement can be general-ized. Gothic architecture was pretty engaged when you think that numerous workmen were willing to spend their whole life building one cathedral. In the twentieth century there were countless socialist building corporations and public housing advocates who worked hard for minimum housing standards for the masses in the interests of the emancipation of the proletariat. The architecture was in both cases an embodiment of an immaterial goal, a window on a better world. Its legitimacy was immeasurably greater than the significance of a single building or the genius of an exalted designer. It reached large sections of the population because it was intended for those large sections. In that sense, the current retro-architecture can also be said to be engaged because it is intended to satisfy the client. However odd it may sound to an outsider, the creation of satisfaction is no mean architectural achievement. And it is indeed an effect that relates to the collective. What this archi-tecture lacks, however, is vision, the utopian moment, the prospect of something better. Which immediately begs the question: can there be engagement without promise? Is populism engaged? Does building for the consumer furnish architecture with a new legitimacy? Is consumer interest a public interest?

It is by now a threadbare truism to say that there are no promises anymore. There are not even any universally accepted values on the strength of which we might intervene in existing situations that call for it. In an age of far-reaching individualiza-tion, collective action and action on behalf of the collective are virtually unfeasible. What and who are to be mobilized? As such, one may well wonder whether the current call for engagement is merely a question of marketing technique. Does the architecture that is concerned with the large scale of the landscape and infrastructure point to social involvement or a search for new customers? Is the architecture that relies on superbly presented statistical research, an honest attempt to embrace various social forces, or is it simply catering cleverly to the short-termism of contemporary politicians and most public commissioning bodies who are only interested in a good story, not in solving problems that take years to prove themselves. Has there really been a shift from engagement originating in inner need to an engagement prompted by the criterion of cultural entrepreneurship which states that architects should pay more attention to what the market requires of them?

It is obvious that when developments are so described, cynicism lurks. Engagement that on closer analysis turns out to be no more than subservience to the market is not true engagement, for it is most certainly not about taking a risk. And it studiously avoids asking why. It is not about society as it should be, but as it is. In this guise, engagement is nothing but a subtle form of opportunism.

But there is another, more daring interpretation possible. The repeated recurrence of the call for engagement is proof that architecture will never be reconciled to the historical loss of its relevance. There exists in architecture a never fully explained resilience which ensures that it always manages to attract the reflective talent that concerns itself with how a disadvantage can be turned into a new advantage. Probably precisely because architecture is specialized in space and space happens to be one of the dimensions of human existence, there is always a task for architecture, in every historical circumstance. Is the architect slowly but surely being sidelined in the rationalized building process? Then a situation arises in which new tasks are so forcefully presented that the rationalized building process is unable to come up with an adequate response. Renewed reflection is what is called for. And ingenious design. Architecture, in other words. It is something Vitruvius discovered, and today's committed architect discovers it too.

Architecture as it fulfils ephemeral requirements with regard to accommodation, real estate and square metres will never be able to develop the necessary vision for the challenges that are even now in the making. A society with new polarizations, for example. Or cities with a majority of foreign-born residents. Or a population that retires en masse. Or human relations that no longer depend on physical proximity. Or a mobility that no longer takes place between A and B, but is A *and* B simultaneously.

Nor will architecture as an arbitrary form of service enable us finally to remove projects that have been on the agenda since time immemorial. The shortage of good-quality housing, for example. Or the extension of the Stedelijk Museum. Or the long-in-the-making North/South metro line in Amsterdam. It is precisely through lack of engagement that these kinds of projects linger on so interminably. Genuine engagement does not deal with things; it gets things done.

The question of space will always be architecture's salvation. But architecture ensures that space will never be just a question of space, but will forever remain a question of vision.

About more, for more
Engaged architectural criticism

Hans Ibelings

Since the turn of the century, 'engagement' has seemed to be busy making a comeback in architecture. Whether there is any actual engagement as yet, I do not know, but it is at any rate a topic of discussion. (This sounds a bit like what Cardinal Alfrink is supposed to have replied when asked when the Second Vatican Council would begin: that it didn't matter so much whether it had already begun, because in retrospect the announcement of the council might well prove to have been more important than the council itself.)

One indication that change is afoot is the growing interest among architects in that which transcends the hyper-individual and in the question of how architecture and urban design might effect the emergence of something communal. Architectural criticism (which is part of the same closed system as architecture) has also witnessed a modest growth of interest in architecture that in some way or other testifies to the social involvement of the designers. In short, there are signs of an as yet indefinable longing among critics and architects for architecture that is more than just attractive, inventive, original and conceptual. In parallel with this, critics have recently begun to question the non-committal nature of their own activities and to wonder whether perhaps too much is published about architecture in which too little is said. These developments, too, could be interpreted as signs of a new engagement. The question is whether or not this engagement will, as so often, be confined to fine words. To be sure, the engagement of critics, who have a self-appointed position on the sideline, seldom goes beyond telling others how things ought to be.

Whatever the case, should the new engagement persist and actually start to amount to something, it would not be such an illogical development. After two decades of post- and supermodernist irony and concomitant detachment, it is time again for a bit more involvement. That's all there usually is to such pendulum swings. As such, the fact that both architecture and architectural criticism are sometimes judged to be pretty lightweight nowadays, and that there appears to be a need for greater seriousness, is only to be expected.

What the response to this light-heartedness might or should entail and what form the engagement might take –

whether in architecture or in architectural criticism – is not entirely clear to me as yet. One thing I do hope, however, is that it will not be a repetition or echo of the last time that architecture and criticism engaged with social and political developments. I do not regard the 1970s as a tempting prospect for the near future. Seldom has there been so much self-righteousness, polarizing rabble-rousing and vilification of anything that did not fit a doctrinaire view of architecture and history. What is more, architecture itself all but disappeared from view, not just among critics and historians, but also, in a rare moment of self-hatred, among architects.

Another thing I hope, incidentally, is that architects do not reacquire the false pretension that architecture can improve society. Nor that architectural critics start believing that architecture, let alone society, can be improved with words, although I fear that many critics have never really abandoned this idea. For even though I have often enough heard fellow critics remark somewhat sniffily that architects do not read but only look at the pictures, the architectural profession is by implication their principal and intended readership. How else is one to interpret the pedantic lectures on what the architect or architecture should be doing? Or all those building reviews in which designers are reprimanded for their shortcomings and praised for the things they have got right according to the schoolmarm critic? Evidently the notion that 'the pen is mightier than the sword' lives on in my profession. I find it all too reminiscent of the madman one used to see at the intersection of Marnixstraat and Rozengracht in Amsterdam, energetically directing the traffic in synch with the traffic lights. He appeared to be genuinely convinced that his arm movements were responsible for stopping and starting the flow of traffic.

Even though I do not believe that critics have the power to direct the architectural traffic, I cling to the idea that they can influence things in a more subtle way: by their choice of topic and choice of audience.

To begin with the latter, critics keen to parade their engagement should in my view do so not by way of the usual moralistic but often oh so non-committal discourses that pass for engagement. In the first place they should do their level best not to preach only to the converted. Even though critics do not always say what their 'parishioners' most want to hear, their sermons are usually aimed at them. As far as I'm concerned, that doesn't mean that souls must be won to swell the ranks of the converted, nor that the voice of the people should be heard more often in architectural criticism in the form of the 'populist' viewpoint that boils down to the claim that architects saddle humanity with products that nobody wants (a viewpoint that oddly enough finds support among otherwise sensible journalists). Engagement might perhaps lie in the modest ambition to use architectural criticism to make the world of architecture more accessible and comprehensible for a wider public than that of insiders. In my view this can be done by looking for other platforms for writing and speaking about architecture than the established media where architecture already has its own little niche.

Furthermore, engagement in architectural criticism can be expressed in the choice of subject matter. It stands to reason that if the architectural pendulum is now swinging in the direction of more engagement, architectural criticism will focus on a different section of architecture than has been the case in recent years. But that is not the whole story, as far as I'm concerned. I suspect that it will above all mean that attention will shift from the very small portion of architecture that has captured the headlines in recent times to a different but equally small portion that will be deemed sensational, important and trendsetting in the next few years.

Nikolaus Pevsner's dictum that 'A bicycle shed is a building; Lincoln Cathedral a piece of architecture' may be oldhat now that almost everybody believes that every building type can be turned into architecture. But even though there may be no typological dividing line between architecture and construction anymore, that is not to say that there is no difference between the small percentage of buildings on which critics confer a right to exist by writing about them, and the many buildings regarded as nondescript and consequently nonexistent in architectural criticism. (Carel Weeber's shrewd definition applies here: it's architecture because it's written about.)

That people should write about trendsetting architecture and that architecture should become trendsetting as a result, is a positive feedback mechanism that is probably unavoidable in architectural criticism and history. What I object to is the automatism with which this results in a great deal being said about precious little, and little or nothing about a great deal. I'm not saying that architectural criticism should be a reflection of building practice (that sounds much too much like positive discrimination). Nor am I in favour of writing about nondescript architecture simply because it is there. But I do think that a great deal of architectural production is too easily dismissed as nondescript by architectural criticism.

Herein lies the chief opportunity for engaged architectural criticism, in my view: through a genuine involvement with the subject of that criticism – architecture – without reducing it to an illustration to an argument or to a neutral backdrop onto which everyone is free to project their own ideas. And without confining the architecture that is worth discussing to that tiny little bit around which nearly all critics so eagerly crowd.

The engaged city

New commitment

Rudi Laermans

We are all prostitutes / Everyone has their price /
And you too will learn to live the lie.
The Pop Group, *We Are All Prostitutes*, 1979

It's an ordinary Saturday afternoon; normally around this time
the city centre slowly starts to fill with thousands of shoppers.
But today, 15 February 2003, it is remarkably quiet along the
central avenues that link the Nord and Midi train stations in
Brussels. They do not seem as dead as the startlingly deserted
streets Eugène Atget once photographed in Paris. The city is
not reduced to its identity as a built environment: there are
some strollers about; here and there people are enjoying the
precocious spring sunshine at a café terrace. But there is no
automobile traffic, which seems to petrify the centre of Brussels
into an unaccustomed silence – as though it did not itself know
what to make of the absence of the mechanized hum it is normally wrapped in. The city has for the moment lost its acoustical
cocoon and seems less urban because of it.

Two hours later, the Avenue Jacqmain, the Place Brouck-
ère, the Avenue Anspach … are filled with the sound of people
and music. Tens of thousands of demonstrators march from the
Nord to the Midi station, many shouting their anger at the naked
invasion of Iraq by the United States. It is a motley collection of
dreadlocks and neatly coiffed heads, the politically engaged and
people protesting for the first time. This is no modern mass: it
does not subscribe to unequivocal anti-imperialist slogans; it is
divided into dozens of subgroups with very different motives for
saying no. The demonstrating mass follows no flag; it symbolizes,
through its presence, merely an *abstract refusal*, for which individual participants, two days later in the Monday newspapers,
give highly divergent reasons.

The gathering is meaningful for every protestor, but taken
as a whole this gives no composite picture of a new ideological
engagement. People have come out to participate and, together
with tens of thousands of other strangers, to say no publicly.
New style engagement is perhaps nothing more than showing
oneself visibly to be engaged, however briefly or noncommittally,
and letting the individual 'no' – or 'yes', it depends on the context
– be subsumed into a temporary collective with no clear identity.
As a rule this occurs within an urban context: cities remain,

even in the era of generalized suburbanization, conductors as well as containers of engagement (I limit this observation to 'the West' – so much ethnocentrism must be conceded, and will continue to set the tone: Brussels is not the world).

'All that is solid melts into air', as Marx and Engels put it in *The Communist Manifesto*. Modern capitalism dissolves all established social relationships, every form of tradition that regulates markets or prices, pacifies power relations, or says who can marry whom under what conditions. It tends to recognize only the temporary contract, legally enforced or not, between individual nomads – between a man and a woman in the private sphere, between an employer and an employee or, more generally, between a seller and a buyer in the economic sphere. Such agreements should in fact not operate in the domain of democratic politics: the citizen is an individual, but in the public sphere he links his personal interest to the common interest by participating in public debates or simply by casting a vote.

Modern democratic politics mark off a magical space in which the private, through the intercession of 'the people' (at election time, but also during social protests, for instance) and rational arguments (debate in parliament and in the open), manages to acquire universal import. This dialectic belief is fast evaporating at the moment: neo-liberal governments address the citizen as a calculating consumer with strictly individual interests, and we've come to behave as such. The implicit, day-to-day belief in the *metaphor* of the market as the sole efficient form of social determination has taken over from the explicit democratic belief. With it vanished, inevitably, and virtually without a sound, the various expressions of ideological utopianism. After all, these invariably banked on a total politicization of society, on a social generalization of the democratic dialectic within the economy as well as education, relations between the sexes as well as those between the old and the young. The most significant blind spot of this utopian faith is now well-known. It presupposed the framework of the modern nation-state; it made absolute the existence of social relationships that were literally bounded and therefore could be centrally organized.

The individual citizen is the central point of address of both modern and postmodern democratic political leaderships, which attempt to achieve legitimacy through an almost endless multiplication of purely administrative monitoring and accountancy procedures, oversight commissions and external audits. However, modern democratic politics was also mass politics, the mobilization of individuals based on interests presented as common by means of ideology and organization, slogans that by now sound simplistic, as well as sometimes widely ramified networks of parties, trade unions, socialized medicine services... Each new expansion of suffrage increased the size of the voting audience to be mobilized and organizationally streamlined, the potential mass of voters who had to be persuaded and led. In the totalitarian politics of fascism, and partly of communism as well, mass democracy turned into a mere technocracy of total mobilization – of total personal engagement in the service of a single ideology and party.

In Brussels in mid-February 2003, I was an elementary particle that along its own orbit unexpectedly encountered tens of thousands of other particles: I was an insignificant atom within a *post-political mass*. The engagement of this mass was real, but it was not sustained by a unified ideology, not circumscribed by a professional network of organizations. About a month later, when the United States had already invaded Iraq, I happened, during a Sunday stroll, upon the modern political mass – which was no longer there. A few hundred protestors, mainly mobilized by the originally Maoist, extreme-left Workers Party voiced an ideological anti-imperialism that apparently could not even persuade hardcore alternative-globalization activists to make the trip to Brussels. Cars drove as usual along the central avenues; the march followed a peripheral route within the Brussels city centre.

Modern political leaders, whether democratic or anti-democratic, relied on the individual citizen but did not trust him. They wanted to educate him and guide him, civilize him and take him by the hand. To this end they mobilized him within collectives, and for this they needed public places, containers that could hold the social currents that were created: streets for marches, squares or large halls for gatherings. Parties and other organizations brought the mass together in the city. This seemed its natural habitat, if only for the obvious concentration of people and institutions, permanent and temporary residents. Yet the culmination of modern mass politics in the form of its anti-democratic counterpart, German fascism, would not have been possible without radio. Fascism mobilized the mass by bringing people together in the streets or in stadiums, and at the same time created a new form of mass politics beyond place through the first post-literary mass medium. It did not broadcast 'the voice of the German people' but instead taught a large part of Germany to listen *simultaneously* to Hitler's voice. Modern mass politics was transformed; it traded the primacy of place and space for that of networks and simultaneity.

In the post-political age, media, including popular mailbases or oft-consulted sites on the Internet, are the primary means to mobilize and channel, to awaken grievances or to express them. Postmodern mass politics are synonymous with the politics of mass-media communications, from which emerge the official power of spin doctors and the unofficial counter-power of alternative computer networks. This makes it possible to mobilize around national as well as global issues: mass-media flows of information have changed the national subject into a world citizen. This explains the surface contingency of publicly expressed engagement and protest movements: the media messages spread by networks may or may not have appeal; they may or may not resonate within the personal sound box of the individualized citizen.

Time plus place, simultaneity of personally resonating information that is in the end connected to a specific place, resulting in a stream of people that temporarily occupied the centre of a capital city and transformed it into a place where engagement was shown, without calling upon a collective political Utopia: on 15 February 2003 Brussels was a *leftover* of modern democratic politics. I was a participant in as well as a witness to a simulacrum, a coalescing of collective grievances within an urban centre induced by the mass-media network space that day after day simultaneously divides and unites individuals within the exclusively virtual collectivity of readers of the same newspaper, listeners to the same radio station, they who watch analogue images on a screen that is by now digital. If one wants to change the world, one must conquer the media and adjust our picture of global society. But such engagement is only 'the capital' part of the formula.

Mobility, *making* culture and society *mobile*, putting into motion and rotating material as well as immaterial things, is *the* trademark of modern capitalism. During the first wave of economic expansion, hundreds of thousands of people moved from the countryside to the city, creating a new urban form, the industrial city, by now a historic patrimony in the West. With the generalization of consumer capitalism that started in the late 1800s, fashion became a primary motor of economic accumulation; precipitating the rapid obsolescence of products, through styling or branding, is incidentally still an excellent guarantee of profit. From the introduction of the famed Ford Model T, mobility itself became a mass consumer item, with well-known negative consequences: massive pollution, massive suburbanization, massive destruction of human lives. It also created a new kind of public event, the fatal car accident, in which the personal intimacy of death has been replaced by the imperceptible speed of an instantly fatal crash.

Mobility now also includes the flows of images and information that circulate throughout the world through mass media and cyberspace. The abstract network space of computer connections irresistibly accelerates the process of globalization and exacerbates the gap between rich and poor, those who are and those who are not connected to the basic infrastructure of today's global society. Yet mobility within cyberspace is at least as important – the continual updating, at a heretofore unimagined rate, of monetary transactions, messages, sites… 'Old news is no news' is a rule we were already familiar with from the regime of mass media, with its monopolies on the production and distribution of information from central points. The network society makes this principle democratic. A site that is not updated regularly, preferably on a daily basis, or a mailbase with few active users, is out for good. We inhabit not a postmodern, but a hypermodern culture.

Mobility usually does not happen by itself; it normally presupposes active mobilization, of money for stock markets as well as of people for products. Modern capitalism has created an ever-growing number of 'mobilizers': fundraisers and consultants within the sphere of capital, product designers and stylists or advertising makers and lifestyle designers within the consumer sphere. These are the familiar examples; in addition there are the legion of laws and regulations that aim to generate activity, that create space at a national and international level, which in principle promote – invariably subject to yet more legal preconditions – the free flow of people, goods and capital. The final element is a culture that idealizes an inconstant and pragmatic character, a flexible and mobile personality or – in the moral register – openness and interest in 'the subject' as well as 'the Other', rewarded with a financial or symbolic bonus. To cling to tradition or the past and to consider the historic identity of a place more important than its future profit potential is seen as nostalgic and dogmatic, if not fundamentalist. This has resulted in a very specific profile for worldwide engagement within the alternative-globalization movement: it merges the traditionally leftist protest against faith in the market metaphor with the conservative call for inertia and 'individuality'. Neo-engagement against neo-liberalism is an ideological oxymoron, and therefore by definition vulnerable.

It's an ordinary Saturday afternoon; Brussels' Rue Neuve is filling up, as is the little section of uptown at the entrance of the stately Avenue Louise. This is where one finds the quintessential modern mass, the *crowd* Walter Benjamin spoke of in his extensive essays and notes about Paris as the 'capital of the nineteenth century'– as a precursor and historical paradigm of modern consumer capitalism. People stroll, usually in twos or in groups, among a virtual collective. The crowd never becomes a real community, because the individual or shared sense of observation is primarily focused on the products in the shop windows. It defines, ultimately, à la Marx and Engels, the global situation; it imbues the Saturday shopping ritual with rhythm. One is a potential buyer, and at the same time one displays, in the clothing and hairstyle worn, an actual consumer history, which often incorporates an explicit meaning for this lifestyle or that subculture.

Besides potential conquests (that is imperialism or globalization), capitalism also colonizes the physical body, the strange zone in which product and individuality coalesce into attractiveness – or not (this is simply everyday reality, without slogans or protest). This place is bewitched, Benjamin also knew that already: he defines fashion at one point as the magical crossing of the anorganic and the organic. It links the fetishism of goods à la Marx with psychological fetishism à la Freud, with the model and the star as mass-media models and the prostitute as an ever-present point of refuge. Yet the transubstantiation of product into flesh only works thanks to the dreams that the first carries, the promises of a life not just comfortable but sensually and erotically successful as well. This imaginary capital is the ultimate power of modern capitalism, the quasi-mythical source from which even the most banal advertising photo draws. We are engaged by a myth that transcends ourselves, because the purchase of a dress, a pair of trousers or a swimsuit seems to provide an ultra-individual happiness, a social surplus of approval. Appearances are deceiving, we know that – yet no argument can stand up to the imaginary truth of one's image in the mirror, the simultaneously contingent and desired reflection, inside a fitting room, of 'me plus this suit'. Identity is identification, and the identification takes place through an image, in both senses of the word: consumer capitalism has colonized our imagination, to the detriment of earlier ideological dream-worlds.

To mobilize, but not politically, has become the dominant design practice. In the sphere of the mass media, entertainment and

consumerism – the distinction is often strictly analytical –
everything is geared to draw attention and stimulate, soothe or
assault the senses. Either it is the register of the pleasant that
dominates: entertaining images and sounds, words that read
smoothly, clothes that feel comfortable – in short, the generalization of muzak as a strategy. The pleasant sensation is nestled
within the familiar; it is recognizable and usually draws on a
stereotype, with or without an ironic twist. Or it is the sensational that rules, the register of the spectacular: beats that
penetrate the body and overwhelm the nervous system, shocking or pulsating images, screaming one-liners and snappy con-
trarian viewpoints – in short the generalization of the strategy
of the showy and the boastful, of the affectedly interesting as
well. Getting attention is giving time, and time is money is
profit, in the short or the medium term.

Consumer capitalism and experience culture now form
two sides of the same coin: we consume experiences (we pay for
them), and we expect soft experiences or instead hard kicks
from what we consume. It is precisely this loop between product
and sensory perception that engages us, and radically – 'down
to the last crumb'. The general identity of the consumer holds
together a more or less fragmented patchwork of individual
identifications; it is the only metaposition left to us in a society
lacking Great Stories (except perhaps that of the environmental
catastrophe – but that is a doom scenario popular with very few
people). This social identity defines us quasi-completely, which
is why we affirm it, albeit out of sheer necessity: the critical or
environmentally aware consumer is a consumer too.

Simultaneously geared toward consumption and experience: this is also the aspect of the architecture of amusement
parks, airports, dance clubs... and shopping centres, of course.
They are abstract non-places, devoid of social or symbolic
identity, built entirely with an eye to the human traffic passing
through. They are also 'mobilizers', artificial places that seduce
and bring together people, producers and conduits of crowds.
Where the crowd is, there also is the product, and both are now
located in settings – the word 'building' suggests too much durability, too much 'permanence' or substance – that offer pleasant
or exciting stimuli. Non-places are often experience machines
as well; they aim to surprise loudly or instead suggest a relax-
ing atmosphere. Their design refers not to general architectural
principles, but rather is guided by the logic of effect and affect:
it is rhetorical; it aims for sensory impressions.

There is a lot that seems doubled now: the motorway by the

information superhighway, the public urban context by the network space, the city itself by the strings of retail outlets, cinema complexes and dance clubs in the no-man's-lands between the historic cities and the suburban enclaves. Cities survive in part thanks to shopping streets, and especially by offering a specific mode of experience: the mix of conviviality and past, of nice cafés or restaurants and historical patrimony. Post-war suburbanization turned the city into an outdated life form, and that is precisely how it has been selling itself for some time now: as a place of interest – as an 'attractor' for people keen to buy and especially people looking for added value. These days, deliberating choosing the city and living there means opting for a special kind of atmosphere, a generator of personal experiences: the city is incorporated into the city feeling. And this can be marketed and sold as well, with slogans like 'Bubbling Brussels' or lofts in old industrial buildings.

The contemporary city feeling is fleeting and nomadic; it attaches itself to many cities – 'this is where I live, that's where I feel at home'. The traditional stroller, so accurately portrayed by Benjamin, was a stay-at-home sort. Day after day he would travel within his own city, seek out the human crowd and gape at the products in the shop windows. The new-style city user lives in Berlin or London, Paris or Amsterdam, but at the same time is an international experience-seeker who prospects actively and compares cities on their experience potential. He is neither traveller nor tourist; he has internalized the identity of consumer so thoroughly that urban variations have merely a personal experience value for him, detached from any concrete history or context. He inhabits a perceptual collage city in which a scrap of Berlin merges seamlessly with a piece of Barcelona or Brussels; he engages himself neither for nor against a city, let alone for or against the Idea of the City: he praises the city only as a consumer.

Engagement and consumerism are now two sides of the same coin: demonstrating or 'doing something political' is a *sign* of engagement that commits one to nothing and nobody; consumerism is an equally non-committal engagement in a lifestyle or subculture, an individual experience or indeed one shared with countless anonymous others – in an ephemeral identity that can be exchanged tomorrow, with no questions or arguments. Does this sound pessimistic? So be it: onward into the future, with or without the city.

Towards a new Utopia

H.J.A. Hofland

If, today, there is an undercurrent of indefinable thinking, a steadily increasing, though as yet not clearly formulated feeling in Western culture – a *Zeitgeist* in the making – it must be the spirit of unease and anxiety. If 'new commitment' is to amount to more than the latest buzzword, we must make an effort to cure the West of that spirit.

In the past half century 'we in the West' have swept ourselves and the rest of the world along in ever-faster progress in all fields: from an increased scientific know-how improving the quality of life, to an unremitting perfection of the art of destruction. Some of the results which affect our daily lives are:

* the growth of urban areas, the spreading megalopolis,
* the concomitant issues of administrative manageability and the vulnerability of public amenities,
* the ongoing change in the nature of work in post-industrial society, the disappearance of jobs for life,
* increased physical mobility, the deficient infrastructure: from congestion to stagnation,
* electronic communication, the vulnerable points being – for the user – the confusing nature of the equipment, anonymous aggression from hackers, susceptibility to viruses, and consequently dependence on the expert, the help desk,
* changing international relations – due to the clash of civilizations or a moral class struggle, or both – resulting, at all events, in terrorism, and, in turn, the quest for new security,
* the realistic threat of intangible dangers: infectious diseases, changes in climate, economic collapse,
* burgeoning consumerism, the birth of a new species of Western Man: the consumer, the supreme omni-user. The planet in the service of entertainment, and news relating to history-in-the-making processed into infotainment. Essentially, the Western consumer lays claim to everything Creation provides. And he acquires more than any of his predecessors in the history of the world. His culture requires it of him. He is obliged to want more, in ever-changing diversity, on pain of self-injury. By wanting more he is expressing his consumer confidence. In that way he ascribes to that requirement.

This occasions a paradox. The consumer – the 'absolute consumer' type – lives, in the all-embracing global revolution, between two fears: the fear that he will miss out and the fear that he will lose everything. The culture and economy of consumption stimulate the former; political, spatial and technical developments promote the latter.

There is a solution. Free him from his desire, his duty to consume, and he will be delivered from his anxiety and fear. This solution is unfeasible, in all respects.

Commitment, in the original sense of the word, means being rationally involved in the world in which one lives, appreciating the human condition and, consequently, taking sides. That commitment enjoyed the relative simplicity of perspicuous social differences. Sides were taken with 'the human being' whom society had deprived, either in his material circumstances or in his dignity, and usually both. Within half a century of growing depoliticization the influence of those differences had been marginalized (assuming they still existed in their earlier form). I do not suppose the term 'commitment' has acquired a different purport, but 'new commitment' means that now, based on current analyses, sides are again being taken in a radically different situation.

To be specific: is the consumer, in his new, desperate plight, a challenge, an invitation to commitment? Can artists and intellectuals feel committed to a society, the objective of which is to develop much into more, in ever-greater variety?

Why not? Experience of the 1990s has proved this substantially. Painters, writers, thinkers, film-makers, architects and urban designers do service to consumerism. The visual artist makes experimental art, the writer concentrates on consumer literature, the film-maker makes reality or virtual reality, the designer specializes in increasing the turnover rate of design, shortens the process from rejuvenation to ageing – and all of that watched over by global mega-corporations. The architect builds fitting accommodation. In the course of the 'Roaring Nineties' the vast majority of the Western creative community had joined the ranks of the 'Land of Cockaigne' employees. Their collective talent serving qualitative and quantitative 'more and ever-more'-enjoyment, in a never-ending succession of absolute satiation, which is the ultimate objective of life in Cockaigne.

If the New Economy, the secret of eternal growth discovered at the end of the last century, had not been an illusion but uncontested reality, that would still (and strictly speaking until the Day of Judgement) have been the content of the commitment of every artist, writer, painter, film-maker, architect. And I think, in the last decade, a 'public' has emerged which will wonder why else artists are on this earth.

Since the end of the New Economy and 11 September 2001 things have changed. But how? And in what respect? A decade of seemingly unlimited growth in unthreatened peace left deep marks; the terrorist attack caused a trauma, the new war and, in particular, its fraught aftermath have perhaps also opened a new perspective of the rest of the world for the masses of the West. But all of this has not produced a revolution; not even the start of one. The economy of consumerism and the concomitant body of behaviour are far too great, too powerful, too deep-rooted for that.

What might a new commitment signify under these circumstances?

There are three clear possibilities.

If we assume that, leaving aside all its manifest shortcomings, Western society in rudimentary form best represents what civilization has to offer, under the current circumstances defence should take highest priority. We should then see the West as a splendid stronghold, surrounded by impenetrable electronic barbed wire with wide welcoming gateways equipped with sensors and ultrapolygraphs – lie detectors with wireless devices recording any malicious intent. And inside this hermetic fence there is an absolutely secure society, in which further perfection is unremittingly pursued on all fronts. There, an archipelago of Disneylands develops, under the creative supervision of 'new commitment'. Green suburbias, shopping malls surrounded by vast parking lots and here and there on the horizon the new high-rise – the headquarters of the Administration, more fanciful, more elegant than those of Frank Gehry's wildest dreams. And all these facilities are connected in a stagnation-free and fail-safe, hacker-proof network. New commitment as the fulfilment of the thraldom serving consumerism. The apotheosis of a defensive architecture (which, as the history of fortress construction demonstrates, can produce great functional and aesthetic achievements).

The second possibility: in Western culture, which has developed first in and through consumerism, an awareness develops in (among) an artistic/intellectual vanguard that we (the hundreds of millions in America and Europe), the heirs of the Enlightenment, have lost our way. To state the obvious. That vanguard exists, that awareness is there. On both sides of the ocean there are countless committed people at work, trying to explain that blind or dogmatic consumerism, with its complex ramifications, is the inside enemy of reason, individual liberty and democracy. They know that the achievements of science and technology cannot be undone. Nostalgia for the pre-electronic era, attempts at de-technologization, are counter-productive. But all the hyper-equipment currently serving consumerism could be put to better use. New commitment implies the willingness of the creative elite to think about a new utopia. That is not revolutionary. In this way the elite restores continuity, once more accepts the function it has performed since the Enlightenment.

The third possibility: revolution. A rebellion like that of the Luddites in England early in the nineteenth century. Those manual workers, who had been made redundant by new textile machinery, smashed everything in the factories to smithereens. Imagine if the masses participating in the consumer culture were to discover the global media industry had been deceiving them for years. An unexpected disaster throws them into an as yet unknown abyss – they would avenge themselves on all the equipment that had replaced true reality with the virtual version. The storming of televisions studios and Disneylands, the day of the Great Camera Burning, et cetera. It would make a good film, thus exhausting this option.

New commitment rests in the second possibility, the outline of a new Utopia in which, in the first instance, those capable of independent thought will break out of the prison into which they, as consumers, have locked themselves.

From shaped space to the making of nothing
Architecture and spatial planning in the late
capitalist Netherlands

Aaron Betsky

Today the Dutch idea of 'maakbaarheid' (makeability) – the
ability of government or shared values to mould an individual
is an outdated and to most people ugly concept. Instead of a
reliance on a government that makes everything better, including the landscape, the wind of free enterprise is blowing over
the polder model. Everyone has to make his own world for
himself, and the only thing government can do is see to it that
all these individual empires are cobbled together in the best
way possible to ensure that not too many conflicts arise. Instead
of creating places and spaces which are public, instead of
trusting that the provision of better housing will create a new
kind of society, but also instead of being confident in the merit
of making more and more land (through poldering) to allow
everyone to live the way he or she wants, the present consensus
is that government must intervene in the inevitable conflict
between those who have the means to secure their own space,
and those who, lacking this possibility, take over the remnants
of public space.[1]

Our society has become one of fences. There are 'Vinex'
developments (suburban new towns) for the new, inward-look-
ing middle-class, busy with the education of their children and
watching television. There little room remains for communal
space.[2] Any space left over is for the homeless or the shiftless,
who need to find temporary work, who hang around or simply
try to survive. Immigrants from cultures oriented to the outside
attempt to take over the street in inner-city areas as public
space, alienating their inward turned neighbours.[3] All the time
more and more space is taken up by the roads needed to get
people to their own well-defined homes or workplaces. Public
space is meant for moving around, not as a place to enjoy .[4]

The government is constantly combating the 'illegal' use
of public space, chiefly because it wants such space to be
either empty, and thus safe, or full of cars. This is a vicious circle:
as we increase our personal isolation public space becomes
increasingly useless and so increasingly neglected and dangerous, and we start to avoid our parks and streets.[5] This change
in our communal spaces has repercussions on the way we
behave towards one another. 'Norms and values', an abstract
and often imposed idea about how we should behave decently

towards one another that is the current buzz word of Dutch politics, is now taking the place of the totally 'makeable' society.[6]

The battle for space, in which places which are public or undefined are taken over, demarcated and privatized, is neither new nor exclusively Dutch. In the United States, for example, the battle for space is central to the way the entire society defines itself: 'Go West, young man' is the adage. The colonization of space on the American continent – and later throughout the world and even the cosmos – but also the centrality of the individual, isolated dwelling in that ever-larger space has propelled the country's economy and culture for more than two centuries. In the United States, public facilities like parks, though often heroically dimensioned, are a side issue.[7]

It is of course easy to use this as a reason to ascribe the breakdown in the belief in a totally makeable society to the influence of America, but the causes of the changes lie deeper.[8] Why, when districts built in the post-war reconstruction period are renovated, is the generous provision of green space and parking facilities, schools and sports centres and other shared facilities, so frequently replaced by houses which are indeed much more spacious, but whose larger size gobbles up every bit of communal space, while what little space remains around the houses is even enclosed by fences from the do-it-yourself shop? Because it sells .[9] Why is new 'nature' created in old polders, and why are few new polders made? Because whatever is not ours must be actually different from space that we have taken over ourselves. Nature, because of its almost holy status, is what guarantees our privatized little worlds: if it is not ours we can accept that it belongs to nobody.[10]

The things that remain, traditional public space, public schools and communal facilities, are increasingly falling into ruin or disappearing because of overdue maintenance. We do use our parks, streets and schools, but we don't really want to pay for them, unless only we can use them. The only thing for which we are prepared to fork over a few bucks is security: we don't want to be annoyed as we move through the remnants of our society's physical space. Technology, in the form of the car in which we isolate ourselves, the cameras which watch over us and the virtual connections which increasingly trap us in their web, is changing physical space into something virtual and invisible, ruled by private companies and totally lacking in reality.[11]

Yet there are still places which we use communally. The new urban public spaces which we actually frequent are shopping centres. Parts of our old inner cities (as in Nijmegen and The Hague) are even being laid out in accordance with the recipe for these enclosed colossuses: you drive to a multi-storey car park through banal surroundings, plunge into the shopping mall, possibly have a bite to eat, then leave again via the same secure concrete transportation warehouse to get back to your safe little house in the Vinex district. Almost everyone does the same thing, so go there on Saturday if you want to find what little remains of society. These quasi-malls are the places where it is still possible to hang around and shop, meet one another and do business. In this manner, we continue to be involved with one another – albeit under the watchful eye of the security services and their cameras.[12]

Outside the town you can find nature preserves, stretches of water and other open areas occupied by the third activity (besides living and working) on which we spend our lives, namely recreation. Recreation is becoming increasingly important now that almost a third of our time is available for us to do we want. Nature is still good for something: for walking or jogging, sailing or windsurfing, cycling or motorcycle racing. The agricultural aspect of the countryside is vanishing, becoming new 'nature', or just somewhere to park your caravan. When government designates large sections of the country as unsuitable for building, it does so to ensure that we can use the space to enjoy nature.[13]

The interesting thing about these places is that in a way they reflect, though in a distorted form, a more traditional form. Just as the Vinex dwelling is a variation on the terrace house, the urban shopping centre is a variation on the old town centre – but not quite. The difference is not just the way in which the architecture tries to imitate the past, so that we feel safer and more at home there, but also the distortion of the activity that takes place there.[14] We less frequently shop because we need to, and more because we enjoy it. On a smaller scale this alienation has already gone a good deal further: we cook because we find it a pleasant recreation, or we eat out. We garden because we like to, not because we need to grow things to eat. We take part in sports instead of engaging in physical labour. On a larger scale this link between 'real' activities and rituals is easily recognisable. Instead of the daily trip in the lift to our desks in the office in the tower block we can scream out our ascent in a roller coaster; instead of returning to the past in a house that belonged to our forefathers, we can simply go to the amusement park. The space that we share provides a clear indication of the nature of the culture that we make collectively.[15]

In this 'experience culture' what matters is not what is 'really' happening or really necessary, but only how much pleasure we can derive from any place or event. In our everyday environment more and more space is being swallowed up by those activities that enable us to create a world we find pleasant and agreeable, but also logical and recognizable. Our spare time is not spent sitting still, but on building our identity by shopping, testing ourselves by participating in sports, imagining a past and perhaps a future for ourselves by visits to historical or cultural facilities, and experiencing a world that still looks natural. Ultimately these are the places that still belong to us all, and every one must be created artificially. The totally makeable society still exists, but all it does now is to make space for experiences that don't demand any commitment.

'Norms and values', or other abstract 'social contracts', are supposed to mitigate this situation.[16] Many of us find this unacceptable, because we believe that we all still live in a world which we need to use communally and fairly. The question is whether we can also accept the new, privatized, paranoid, uncommitted reality and make something of it, instead of just grumbling about it. One possibility would be to allow the spaces to develop into authentic experience (or the experience of authenticity) instead of just something to live through. This would mean that what we look at or what we do in our spare time makes us understand where and who we are. The important thing here is to experience a world that is greater than ourselves which is also a world we might be able to change, though only by working together as part of a greater whole. Instead of making polders we could realise that the polders could also be made differently. Instead of the totally makeable town, district or dwelling, the issue would be one of totally makeable public space, which would be the property of everyone and no one, capable of being experienced in a wide range of different ways.[17]

The first step in this process would be to represent and reflect the world around us. The beginning of the 1990s saw a radical change in the Netherlands in the way people thought about urban sprawl. A few designers and planners wanted not only to retain existing landscape structures, but also to make them visible. Between Prinsenland (1988) and Leidsche Rijn (1998) what I would call the Rotterdam School of urban planners (including people such as Riek Bakker, Frits Palmboom, Kees Christiaanse and Joost Schrijnen) thought up ways of, while not completely retaining or copying new subdivisions, original agricultural patterns, building elements and forestation, integrating those historic elements with new construction in such a way that people become aware of what is new and what is old: people can see what has been newly built and when it was built.[18] Sometimes, as with the sheep meadows between the terrace houses of the Langerak neighbourhood of Leidsche Rijn, this tactic takes a rhetorical turn, but it remains a collage of old and new in which open space is used to hold up a mirror to what is made by human beings.

There are also many Dutch artists who see it as their task to portray this strange new world. Recent Dutch photography hardly does anything else. Instead of portraying the world minutely or heroically, like the Becher School, photographers like Frank van der Salm, Rineke Dijkstra and Bas Princen, to name three at random, make images which mainly reflect the space around us. We are conscious of the fact that we, like the people and buildings in the photos, are on our own. Sometimes we even realize that these spaces are artificial, or in any event unreal. None of this makes the image itself any more real – it is only a photo, or sometimes even a projection – but it does increase our awareness of that unreality.[19]

With computer technology everything can be made different. We can make spaces we never knew were possible.[20] Outside the Netherlands, but also in the work of certain Dutch architects whose work can exist only through and sometimes in digital media, the result is often a new world, full of strange shapes, completely outside our experience, and difficult to copy in 'meatspace'. The post-OMA School (perhaps comparable with the post-Becher school), however, has many disciples who see it as their task to transform reality in such a way as to explore new areas of experience. Sometimes, as in the plans of the architect Raoul Bunschoten, the scale of the new space is regional, but even the small communal spaces in MVRDV's housing projects provide an example of such an aim. If it is true that with a computer everything can be different, then the task these architects take on is to allow us to see and experience what kind of spatial experiences that offers.[21]

What is often missing in this work is space itself. Because photographers' portraits and architects' works are commissioned, there is little scope for reflection. This task is reserved for art.[22] In art reality is pushed aside, allowing us to discover something in the empty canvas, on the white surface or in the abstract shape that does not presently exist. This is a continuing theme in the modernism of the past century. If there is one thing that we can learn from artists, it is that it is precisely this essential emptiness, this significant but meaningless nothingness, that can be so important in a densely populated country such as the Netherlands.[23] Only when a piece of ground cannot be inhabited, used or experienced, when we can only discover it, will we come to realise where we are and what we can (and can not) achieve .[24]

At present this sort of space can only be found in leftover or peripheral areas. The 'Tweede Maasvlakte' (a sandy area where Rotterdam's newest harbour expansion is under construction in what used to be the sea) is a heroic ode to emptiness and potential, but even small, leftover bits of urban ground, where a property has been demolished or where an intersection makes any sort of building impossible, have a bit of nothing to offer. They are not part of nature, nor indeed do they belong to anyone. Sadly such examples of emptiness are almost always temporary: a new container port is bound to be built in the 'Maasvlakte', a new building will surely occupy the valuable bit of empty real estate, or a landscape architect will prettify the intersection. Perhaps this is appropriate, given that perception, too, is time-dependent. Now these are places that are also used for illegal parties and other, more personal or pornographic, activities, so creating a kind of (uncommitted) community.[25] But if we want to make a communal experience out of the spaces that join us to one another and to our reality – and I believe this is the best we can hope for – then we will have to think up ways in which this precious nothingness can be fixed in space and time.

Notes

1   A great supporter of this view is Wim Derksen, Director of the Netherlands Institute for Spatial Research. See Wim Derksen, 'Het Einde van de Ruimtelijke Ordening', *Ruimte in Debat*, no. 1, 2003, pp. 2-11.

2   For a description of these developments, see H. van Rossum, F. van Wijk, L. Baljon, *De stad in uitersten: Verkenningstocht naar Vinex-land*, NAi Publishers, Rotterdam 2001.

3   Cf. *Smaken verschillen: multicultureel bouwen en wonen*, Ministry of Housing, Spatial Planning and the Environment – Advisory board 032, 2002. The idea that the city is an 'arena of conflict' in which possession is the central issue, is discussed at length by Edward Soja in *Postmodern Geographies. The Reassertion of Space in Critical Society*, Verso, London 1989, in particular pp. 138-156.

4   This is the opinion of Francine Houben and the theme of Rotterdam's first International Architecture Biennial, held in 2003. See Francine Houben, Luisa Maria Calabrese (ed.), *Mobility: A Room with a View*, NAi Publishers, Rotterdam 2003.

5   Cf. Maarten Hajer, Arnold Reijndorp, *In search of a new public domain. Analysis and strategy*, NAi Publishers, Rotterdam 2001, p. 53.

6   This was certainly the case put forward by the murdered Dutch politician Pim Fortuyn, when he argued that the old city should be

retained, safeguarded and not subjected to further expansion. He believed that social cohesion must come about as the result of communal standards and imposed values. See Pim Fortuyn, *De puinhopen van acht jaar Paars*, Karakter Uitgevers, Rotterdam 2002.

7   Cf. J.B. Jackson, *Landscapes in Sight*, Yale University Press, New Haven 1977; Mike Davis, *The Ecology of Fear. Los Angeles and the Imagination of Disaster*, Metropolitan Books, New York 1998; Soja, op. cit., note 3.

8   According to Ulrich Beck the change was brought about by 'reflexive modernism', a condition in which we are constantly searching for circumstances in which the risks we run are acceptable. See Ulrich Beck, *Risk Society. Towards a New Modernity*, Sage Publications, London 1992. Henri Lefebvre (*The Production of Space*, Blackwell Publishers, Cambridge 1974) also believes that the conflict over space is an essential component of our society.

9   This is confirmed by a report commissioned by Amstelland MDC, and carried out by Motivaction, 'Het Grote Woonwensenonderzoek', 2002.

10   Cf. Tracy Metz, *De Nieuwe Natuur. Reportages over een veranderend landschap*, Ambo, Amsterdam 1998. For a history of the man-made landscape, see J.G. Berkhout et al. (ed.), *Het land van Holland*, Amsterdam Historical Museum, Amsterdam 1978.

11   See Beck op. cit., note 8, and Manuel Castells, *The Rise of the Network Society*, Malden Press, Oxford 1996.

12   The shopping-oriented world was recently described at length in Rem Koolhaas et al. (ed.), *The Harvard Guide to Shopping*, Taschen Publishers, Cologne 2000.

13   Cf. Tracy Metz, *Fun! Leisure and Landscape*, NAi Publishers, Rotterdam 2002.

14   Cf. Michael Sorkin, *Variations on a Theme Park*, Verso, London 1995.

15   I have attempted to describe these changes in *Icons: Magnets of Meaning*, San Francisco Museum of Modern Art, San Francisco 1999.

16   This is not a new phenomenon. Abram de Swaan (*Zorg en de staat. Welzijn, onderwijs en gezondheidszorg in Europa en de Verenigde Staten in de nieuwe tijd*, Bert Bakker, Amsterdam 1989), signalled such a 'civilising offensive' as far back as the end of the nineteenth century.

17   This is the basic principle of 'culturally based planning', a relatively new concept developed by Bernard Colenbrander, Willem Oomens and others, which is now increasingly being used as a basic principle when thinking about the preservation of monuments and historic buildings and the role of government in public space.

18   There is still no description of this 'school', which came together to work on Prinsenland. For background about its ideas see Frits Palmboom, *Rotterdam, verstedelijkt landschap*, 010 Publishers, Rotterdam 1987.

19   In 2003 this way of working was the subject of an exhibition organised by Linda Vlassenrood in the Netherlands Architecture Institute. See Linda Vlassenrood (ed.), *Reality Machines. Mirroring the every-*

day in contemporary Dutch architecture, photography and design, NAi Publishers, Rotterdam 2003.

20   Walter Benjamin has already observed that these spaces were also discovered by an earlier technology, that of the camera, in his 'The Work of Art in the Age of Mechanical Reproduction', in: *Illuminations*, Schocken Books, New York 1969, pp. 217-252, p. 236: 'The enlargement of a snapshot does not simply render more precise what in any case was visible, though unclear: it reveals entirely new structural formations of the subject.'

21   Raoul Bunschoten makes use of these possibilities in his project for the province of North Brabant, in which various computer-based scenarios are developed for the region. In '3D City' and '4D City' and also in their 'Functionmixer', MVRDV investigate the possibilities offered by three-dimensional computer simulation for urban analysis and planning.

22   The place of abstraction in art is perhaps also suggested by its architecture: see Brian O'Doherty, *Inside the White Cube. The Ideology of the Gallery Space*, University of California Press, Berkeley 1999.

23   Manfredo Tafuri saw the fact that architecture could only produce 'the empty sign' as negative, but his analysis can also be turned round: the meaningless sign can also be seen as the tomb of the capitalist drive to factionalism and semiotics. Cf. Manfredo Tafuri, *Architecture and Utopia. Design and Capitalist Development*, The MIT Press, Cambridge (Mass.) 1992, pp. 150ff.

24   The perception of the infinitely new, which could lead to a changed perception of the place of living human beings in reality was an effect formerly reserved for monuments and tombs, as Richard Etlin explains: 'There we feel that condition as an alternative mode of our own condition, not dispersed, but rather confined within a negative image of our own positive form, it offers a possibility of hope or consolation, or, at the very least, understanding.' Richard Etlin, *Symbolic Space. French Enlightenment Architecture and Ideology*, The University of Chicago Press, Chicago 1994, p. 198. On the other hand this perception can also be seen as the acme of modern (or postmodern) art: 'The postmodern would be that which in the modern puts forward the unpresentable in presentation itself: that which denies itself the solace of good form, the consensus of a taste which would make it possible to share collectively the nostalgia for the unattainable ; that which reaches for new presentations, not in order to enjoy them but in order to impart a strong sense of the unpresentable.' Jean-François Lyotard, *The Postmodern Condition. A Report on Knowledge*, University of Minnesota Press, Minneapolis 1984, p. 154.

25   I have investigated these spaces in my *Queer Space. The Spaces of Same-Sex Desire*, William Morrow, New York 1996. See also Albert Pope, *Ladders*, Princeton Architectural Press, New York 1998, pp. 226 et seq., for an analysis of the possibility of such spaces in the dispersed city, and Hajer/Reijndorp, op. cit., note 5, p. 128.

Art after the end of history

New commitment

It would seem the existence of commitment in contemporary art is something to be surprised about. Otherwise we would not refer to *new* commitment. Yet it is hard to pinpoint the exact nature of that surprise at the so-called new commitment in the arts. Does it mean there is *once more* commitment in the arts? That commitment has made a come-back in the arts? Is it surprising that things recur, that in art there is a coming and going of themes? And is it indeed true – as would seem to be surmised – that commitment has ever been absent? Or is it surprising that commitment in the arts is returning *now*, of all times – if it actually is? And how should we describe that "now", so that the return of commitment in the arts might indeed be surprising? For adherents of Fukuyama's theory on the end of history, the return of commitment in the arts merely attests, for now, to bourgeois boredom.

The end of history should not, according to Fukuyama, be seen as the untenable assertion that no more great, shocking and gripping events might occur, or that no more wars might break out, but as the proposition that we will keep on arriving at capitalist liberal democracy as the system that best meets man's desire for recognition.[1] So capitalist liberal democracy marks the end of history, conceived as the development of politico-social thinking, not as a succession of political and social events. Accordingly, in a country that was once a liberal democracy, an authoritarian regime may seize power, but such developments cannot but be seen as a relapse into a primitive form of social organization and are bound ultimately to prove untenable. Fukuyama is convinced that the mere existence of the idea of liberal democracy will ultimately enable it to triumph over actual systems which are at variance with it. No single actual politico-social system can withstand the idea of liberal democracy. In other words, in a world in which a great many countries still do not have liberal democracy, the very idea of such a democracy is an irresistible inducement for – sure enough – resistance. And once liberal democracy has been installed in those countries, resistance to it is almost impossible, or at all events doomed to be the loser in the light of history.

True, Fukuyama does admit that it is possible to detect imperfections, sometimes even glaring deficiencies in existing liberal democracies. But all those imperfections and deficiencies can, he believes, be remedied within the formal framework of liberal democracy. Consequently, resistance within liberal democracies today can only comprise reformist ambitions or, in countries where there is no liberal democracy, would have to be in the form of a demand for such. Resistance could only be along the lines of attempts to deploy reforms and thus enable actual democracies to meet the ideals of a liberal democracy as best as they can, or else attempts to replace aristocratic, despotic or communist regimes by liberal democracies. Fukuyama might be expected to envisage a role, after the end of history, for artistic commitment – assuming it had reformist ambitions. However, he is so convinced of the perfection of capitalist liberal democracy that he can only spare some less than flattering explanations for the fact that capitalist liberal democracies actually have moments of instability. Perfection, according to Fukuyama, is so dull that there will always be people who, purely from boredom, will want something else, without properly realizing that they want something that is not necessarily better than what they know.

> (…) supposing that the world has become 'filled up', so to speak, with liberal democracies, such that there exist no tyranny and oppression worthy of the name against which to struggle? Experience suggests that if men cannot struggle on behalf of a just cause because that just cause was victorious in an earlier generation, then they will struggle *against* the just cause. They will struggle for the sake of struggle. They will struggle, in other words, out of a certain boredom: for they cannot imagine living in a world without struggle. And if the greater part of the world in which they live is characterized by peaceful and prosperous liberal democracy, then they will struggle *against* that peace and prosperity, and against democracy.[2]

In Fukuyama's opinion May '68 was nothing other than the product of bourgeois boredom. The vogue of 'terrorism chic', which, coincidentally, was all the rage around 9/11 (in the 2002 spring collection of the Belgian designer Raf Simons or in Terry Richardson's 'Sabotage' photo reportage for *The Face* magazine), would have undoubtedly been something he considered to be (unacceptable) trendy confirmation of his theory. Is the catwalk not the prime place to come up with something after the end of history, and for that very reason the models all parade with such an air of boredom? And is the flirtation with terrorist and militarist aesthetics not the way for fashion to overcome its

intrinsic boredom? After all, for Fukuyama, after history has
ended there will only be room for empty formalism in art and,
consequently, in the applied arts.

> Artists like to convince themselves that they are being socially
> responsible in addition to being committed to aesthetic values.
> But the end of history will mean the end, among other things,
> of all art that could be considered socially useful, and hence the
> descent of artistic activity into the empty formalism of the
> traditional Japanese arts.[3]

Fukuyama's objection to the post-historical position of art –
incidentally the only reflection on art in *The End of History and
the Last Man* – is, as he himself intimates, taken straight from
a well-known footnote in Alexandre Kojève's reading of Hegel on
the disappearance of man at the end of history. In the footnote
Kojève explains that he initially recognized in the 'American
way of life' the foreshadowing of life in the post-historical period,
but that he changed his mind after a trip to Japan in 1959.

> Post-historical Japanese civilization has committed itself in
> ways that are diametrically opposed to the 'American way'.
> No doubt Japan no longer had Religion, Morals or Politics in
> the 'European' or 'historical' sense of these words. But the
> purest *Snobbism* has created negativistic disciplines out of
> the 'natural' or 'animal' experience which were far more effec-
> tive than those proceeding – in Japan or elsewhere – from
> 'historical action', i.e. military and revolutionary conflicts or
> forced labour.[4]

Nô theatre, the tea ceremony and Ikebana flower arranging may
be upper-class privileges, yet all Japanese people are able to live
in accordance with completely formalized values, values that
are entirely free of any 'human' content in the 'historical' sense
of the word. Kojève gives the example of entirely 'gratuitous'
suicides, be they by the traditional samurai sword or kamikaze
missions using aircraft or torpedo boats. Clearly Kojève could
not suspect that, after 9/11, the kamikaze pilot would be the
perfect incarnation of the conflict he predicted between the historical and post-historical worlds, and perhaps, even less, that
he would not be a 'post-historical', but a 'historical' character.
Fukuyama, like Kojève, is of the opinion that there is no
place whatsoever in present-day capitalist liberal democracy for
artistic commitment, either in the reformist or revolutionary
sense of the word, but not as intra-systemic or anti-systemic

resistance either. Ikebana is felt to be the model for contemporary Western artistic practice and some forms of design closely approach that. The architect, too, who feels duty bound to add trendy logos to ponderous liberal-democratic institutions, is actually embracing Fukuyama's Ikebana-philosophy of art, despite all the rhetoric refuting it. Consequently, it is somewhat ironic that in 2003 Rem Koolhaas was the winner – obviously deservedly, by the way – of the 15th 'Praemium Imperiale' of the Japan Art Association. Kojève, who, after the Second World War, had given up his professoriate of philosophy in favour of a career as an official in the European Commission, would undoubtedly have been extremely pleased with Koolhaas's much-discussed proposal for a new European logo – the so-called 'barcode flag'.[5] After all, with Koolhaas's logo, which aims, with branding advice, to solve the problems of representation occasioned by the muddled, confederal character of the European Union, the formalism of Ikebana has, as Kojève predicted, eventually become the model for artistic practice. The role of the artist, or architect in this case, entails, at best, 'expressing' and shaping politics. Prodi is for AMO a client, just as PRADA is. When the end of history is past, art and politics meet, in discussions on the form of a multicoloured 'flag'.

But Fukuyama and Kojève are mistaken. May '68 constituted such an enormous infringement of the belief in the capitalist system that capitalism itself was forced to review Fordian philosophy. If capitalism is still standing today, it is entirely thanks to the way it has succeeded in boosting this system since then. Far from being entirely superfluous at the end of history, artistic commitment has itself become the model for all forms of labour in the capitalist system. Far from art being a purely formalistic supplement to capitalist liberal democracy, capitalism has discovered in artistic commitment a spiritual supplement or *supplément d'âme*.

In *Le nouvel esprit du capitalisme* Luc Boltanski and Eve Chiapello present an analysis of what they term the third spirit of capitalism.[6] They show how the current management debate which is essential for the spirit of new capitalism amounts to salvaging and recycling values which reigned supreme in the artistic commitment of the sixties. In their view, capitalism survived May '68 by integrating its values. Their analysis proceeds from a minimal definition of capitalism as a principle focusing on the infinite accumulation of capital using means which are theoretically peaceful. Only capitalists, i.e. those who have a surplus of the necessities of life, can comply with that principle.

Those who do not have that surplus at their disposal sell their labour and relinquish the right to sell the products of their labour – a right to which the owners of the means of production are entitled. So paid labour is the reverse side of capitalism. Capitalism is, according to Boltanski and Chiapello, in principle an absurd system for both types of participants.

> Capitalism is, in many respects, an absurd system: wage-earners have lost the ownership of the results of their labour and the possibility of leading active lives outside their subordination. As for the capitalists – they are prisoners of an endless, insatiable process, which is totally abstract and dissociated from the satisfaction of consumption needs, even if they are a luxury. For both types of protagonists inclusion in the capitalist process is impossible to justify.[7]

In other words: capitalism as such can motivate few people to subscribe to the capitalist system. Capitalist commitment depends on the body of arguments which can be invoked to demonstrate the individual and collective advantages of participation in capitalist processes. In a reference to Max Weber's *Die protestantische Ethik und der Geist des Kapitalismus*, they call the ideology legitimizing capitalist commitment 'the spirit of capitalism'. They follow Louis Dumont in using the word 'ideology' for the body of shared beliefs as recorded in institutions and acknowledged in deeds, in actions, and as such embedded in reality.[8] So the spirit of capitalism is the ideology that legitimizes the reason for people to subscribe to capitalism, individually or collectively, which as such is simply absurd. Boltanski and Chiapello take from Max Weber the idea that people need important moral reasons to wish to subscribe to capitalism. According to Weber, the belief that duty was primarily the practising of a profession in the world became accepted during the Reformation. The conception of labour as a *Beruf* or profession – in other words, a kind of lay version of a religious calling – provided the merchants and entrepreneurs of emerging capitalism with a normative foothold and the necessary psychological motivation to dedicate themselves ceaselessly and dutifully to their task, to proceed with rationalizing their affairs which is necessary to generate maximum profit – profit which signals success in their particular 'calling'. Boltanski and Chiapello derive from Albert Hirschman the idea that not only is capitalism incapable of existing without individual moral grounds, but that it cannot exist either without justifications in terms of the common good.[9] According to Hirschman the eighteenth-century elite did not primarily value lucrative activities because of the personal advantage they expected, but because of the socio-political advantages those activities were thought to comprise. The pursuit of profit became the passion to top all others. However, unlike Weber, Boltanski and Chiapello did not seek to describe the genesis of capitalism, but a transformation in the spirit of capitalism since the 1960s. It is, of course, possible to refer to traditional arguments from the economic sciences to describe the present-day spirit of capitalism. Obviously, material progress, efficiency in the satisfaction of needs and the compatibility of capitalism with liberal political systems are components of the spirit of capitalism, but according to Boltanski and Chiapello these arguments are too general to really motivate people, with their concrete living circumstances, to subscribe to capitalism. If people are to be properly 'sensitized', a different debate is needed than that of the economic sciences. In their view since the nineties it has been the management debate, primarily focusing on the so-called 'executive staff' or management:

> This debate mainly addresses managers whose adhesion to capitalism is especially indispensable for the running of the business and the creation of profit, but whose high level of commitment cannot be obtained by mere force. They are less bound by necessity than the workers, can oppose passive resistance, not get reservedly committed, undermine the capitalist order by criticizing it from within. There is also a risk that the children of the middle classes who are the almost natural source of management recruitment will 'defect', as A. Hirschman put it (1972) and head for professions which are less integrated in the capitalist process (the liberal professions, arts and sciences, public services) or even partially withdraw from the labour market – the more so, the more varied the resources at their disposal educational, hereditary and social).[10]

The impact of the spirit of '68 has meant that people nowadays prefer professions which offer scope for development, permit creativity and provide a degree of autonomy, and so on. Intrinsic motives do offset extrinsic motives and that, in turn, is clearly affected by the hereditary, educational and social resources which growing numbers of young people can fall back on. Be it as it may, authenticity, creativity and autonomy are important factors in the agendas of the middle class (and its young people) from which not only the arts recruit but are also natural 'suppliers' of managers. If the profit sector wishes to retain its competitive position compared with the arts in the recruitment of human resources, it will have to offer candidate managers what they might well be seeking otherwise in the non-profit arts sector. The neo-management debate which is a key element in the spirit of new capitalism – the spirit, as we have seen, that people must motivate to subscribe to the capitalist system – will give values like creativity and autonomy an important place. In the neo-management jargon of the 1990s, the manager is not someone who 'motivates' his staff, because that would mean motivation is extrinsic. In current management 'philosophy' the company is not the place where I become estranged from myself, but the place where I can be myself. Slavoj Zizek gives the example of hackers who are called in by computer and software companies:

> Paradigmatic here are the 'postmodern' hackers-programmers, these extravagant eccentrics hired by large corporations to pursue their programming hobbies in an informal environment. They are under the injunction to be what they are, to follow their innermost idiosyncrasies, allowed to ignore social norms of dress and behaviour (they obey only some elementary rules of polite tolerance of each other's idiosyncrasies); they thus seem to realize a kind of proto-Socialist Utopia of overcoming the opposition between alienated business, where you earn money, and the private hobby-activity that you pursue for pleasure at weekends. In a way, their job is their hobby, which is why they spend long hours at weekends in their workplace behind the computer screen.[11]

However, the apparent Utopia has a subtle drawback. The more my company gives me room to be myself, the more I am expected to identify with 'my company'. After all, I only work for my company because I myself want to. But if *I* am the one who wants to work for this company, I can hardly contradict my employer. I would, after all, be contradicting myself. This double bind illustrates the way in which capitalism has managed to turn the critical potential of a certain artistic criticism to its own advantage. The stratagem used by capitalism is that in the course of the last thirty years it has taken seriously the employees' complaints that they wanted to 'develop'. However, the interpretation that the term 'self-development' has gradually acquired might cynically be described as 'having the chance to work, of one's accord, more and with greater motivation, for a lower wage'. The employee of today is expected to... *commit himself* to his company. And that means wages are not the prime motive for work, or even play no part whatsoever.

We may be surprised at what would seem to be 'new commitment' in the arts, but the primary locus of commitment these days is the *company*: employees are the ones who commit themselves, or are expected to commit themselves to their company. Or else the company meets its commitments, or occasionally enters into a 'new commitment' vis-à-vis its employees. A 'new commitment' of that type generally means that even more is expected from the employees, without that necessarily being compensated by an increase in wages. Consequently, commitment is no longer an adequate collective term for *certain* activities – artistic or not – which are directed *against* the capitalist system or certain aspects of it; no, commitment from now on is the term for *all* activities *within* the capitalist system. 'New commitment' may be intended in the title of this book as a collective term for all manner of artistic resistance to the capitalist system or certain aspects of it, but it would be a perfect description of the present-day logic of the system itself that artistic resistance is contesting.

Even the assembly line, for so long the veritable incarnation of detested Taylorism, today would appear to be a place surreptitiously brimming with creativity, at least if we are to believe the commercial for the Citroën Xsara Picasso. At all events, Toyotaism is known to ascribe more 'responsibility', more 'autonomy' to the individual worker than Fordism did, making the assembly-line worker feel less alienated. So commitment is expected even from the assembly-line worker – and that is pretty new. The Japanification of the world which Kojève, who died in 1968, believed he perceived at the end of history, did not assume the form of formalization after 1968, but of 'responsabilization', not of design but of deontology.

> Toyotaism (…) served as a base for rejecting the legacy of Fordism and turning (…) production methods 'back to front'. The workers, from then on known as *operators*, gradually found themselves to be in charge of quality control and certain maintenance operations. (…) The workers were considered to be the winners in these organizational changes, less 'alienated' than they had been before, since they had become fully responsible for some products, their work had been 'enriched', they were rid of the minor bosses and had more opportunities to obtain amenities to enable them to perform their duties.[12]

Since the 1960s the spirit of capitalism has, in this way, experienced an impressive mutation, partly thanks to the artistic criticism of the 60s. The capitalist protagonist is no longer the 'owner' or the 'director', but the 'manager'. Present-day management and the personage of the present-day manager are the products of the way a certain artistic debate has latched onto traditional capitalism. If we are to see the manager as the prime character in the artistic transformation of capitalism since the sixties, it might be easier to envisage the curator as the prime character of the capitalistic transformation of art since the 60s. After all, the curator is merely a manager (of artistic processes), and in some cases a manager – when a company is in difficulties – is invited to act as a curator (of economic processes). In the personage of the manager/curator, art and capitalism have become mutually integrated. This has far-reaching consequences for what commitment in the arts can mean today. If capitalism has become a matter of commitment, art today has only one possible way of committing itself, that is *not* to commit itself. After all, if the artist sees his commitment as anti-systemic resistance, he can only commit himself by 'exiting', even though it is not always clear how that suggestion by Antonio Negri and Michael Hardt to 'exit' should actually be effectuated.[13] At all events, it is far from evident that 'new commitment', when apparent in established institutions, networks, galleries, festivals, biennials and so on, will want to be apparent without calling into question the extent to which the arts sector adheres to capitalist beliefs. If someone opts to operate within the arts sector, he or she is almost bound to sabotage the whole thing. The philosopher (from Belgium) cannot wear clogs (from Holland), so must stick to asking awkward questions.

One might wonder, for instance, what mega-commitment is undertaken vis-à-vis 'committed' art when 'new commitment' is referred to in the arts. One of the effects of this debate is that artists who are covered by the 'new commitment' label will receive the necessary exposure, in monographs, reviews, discussions, interviews. Consequently, the artists of new commitment will be talked about in the years to come, and that is the best thing that can happen to them, in marketing terms. Some informed cynicism is required to embellish on this prediction: there will be more attention for the artists of the new commitment than for everything they are committed to. Accordingly, the debate on new commitment in the arts will have to assume the structure of a performative paradox: the exposure generated by the debate on new commitment for alleged new commitment in art, will proceed according to the marketing techniques of new capitalism, which new commitment actually frequently brings into question. In that respect we can extend our original prediction even further. If new commitment is indeed committed to its criticism of the capitalist conditions in which it has to work, it will not submit passively to that paradoxical logic and will be forced to cause breakdowns at all the levels at which it operates. Artists will ask themselves if the intention of new commitment is to subdue, by cataloguing, documenting, publishing, promoting and selling it (New! Art and Architecture from Holland! Now contains commitment!). Committed amazement about new commitment in the arts assumes an awareness that the entire transparent box of tricks for marketing thinking on art is no longer spent on new commitment – and that is the very reason why we can term such commitment 'new'. Perhaps new commitment is new because there is nothing it detests more than the most capitalist of all possible designations: 'new'!

Notes

1 See Francis Fukuyama, *The End of History and the Last Man*, Penguin Books, London 1992.

2 Idem, p. 330.

3 Idem, p. 320.

4 'La civilisation japonaise "post-historique" s'est engagée dans des voies diamétralement opposées à la "voie américaine". Sans doute, n'y a-t-il plus eu au Japon de Religion, de Morale, ni de Politique au sens "européen" ou "historique" de ces mots. Mais le Snobisme à l'état pur y créa des disciplines négatrices du donné "naturel" ou "animal" qui dépassèrent de loin, en efficacité, celles qui naissaient, au Japon ou ailleurs, de l'Action "historique", c'est-à-dire des Luttes guerrières et révolutionnaires ou du Travail forcé.' Alexandre Kojève, *Introduction à la lecture de Hegel*, (*Leçons sur la Phénomenologie de l'Esprit professées de 1933 à 1939 à l'Ecole des Hautes Etudes* collected and published by Raymond Queneau), Gallimard, Paris 1947, p. 437 n.

5 See, for instance, *The New York Times*, 23 May 2002.

6 See Luc Boltanski and Eve Chiapello, *Le nouvel esprit du capitalisme,* Gallimard, Paris 1999; also Eve Chiapello, *Artistes versus managers. Le management culturel face à la critique artiste,* Métailié, Paris 1998.

7 'Le capitalisme est, à bien des égards, un système absurde: les salariés y ont perdu la propriété du résultat de leur travail et la possibilité de mener une vie active hors de la subordination. Quant aux capitalistes, ils se trouvent enchaînés à un processus sans fin et insatiable, totalement abstrait et dissocié de la satisfaction de besoins de consommation, seraient-ils de luxe. Pour ces deux genres de protagonistes, l'insertion dans le processus capitaliste manque singulièrement de justifications.' Luc Boltanski and Eve Chiapello, op. cit., note 6, p. 41.

8 See Louis Dumont, *Homo hierarchicus,* Gallimard, Paris 1966.

9   See Albert Hirschman, *Exit, Voice and Loyalty,* Harvard University Press, Cambridge (Mass.) 1970.

10 'Ce discours s'adresse en priorité aux cadres, dont l'adhésion au capitalisme est particulièrement indispensable à la marche des entreprises et à la formation du profit, mais dont le haut niveau d'engagement requis ne peut être obtenu par la pure contrainte et qui, moins soumis à la nécessité que ne le sont les ouvriers, peuvent opposer une résistance passive, ne s'engager avec réticence, voire miner l'ordre capitaliste en le critiquant de l'intérieur. Le risque existe également que les enfants de la bourgeoisie, qui constituent le vivier quasi naturel de recrutement des cadres, fassent défection, selon l'expression de A. Hirschman (1972), en se dirigeant vers des professions moins intégrées au jeu capitaliste (professions libérales, art et science, service public), ou même se retirent partiellement du marché du travail, et cela d'autant plus qu'ils disposent de ressources diversifiées (scolaires, patrimoniales et sociales).' Idem Boltanski and Chiapello refer here to the above book by Hirschman which was published in French in 1972 under the title *Face au déclin des entreprises et des institutions,* (translation. C. Beysseyrias), Les Editions ouvrières, Paris.

11 Slavoj Zizek, *The Ticklish Subject. The Absent Centre of Political Ontology,* Verso, London/New York 1999, p. 368.

12 '(...) le toyotisme (...) a servi de point d'appui pour rejeter l'héritage du fordisme et 'penser à l'envers' (...) les méthodes de productions. Les ouvriers, que l'on appelle désormais des *opérateurs,* se voient peu à peu chargés du contrôle de qualité et de certaines opérations de maintenance. (...) Les ouvriers sont censés sortir gagnants de ces changements organisationnels, moins "aliénés" qu'ils ne l'étaient auparavant, puisqu'ils deviennent responsables à part entière de certaines productions, que leur travail s'en trouve 'enrichi', qu'ils sont libérés des petits chefs autoritaires et ont plus de facilités pour obtenir des aménagements facilitant l'accomplissement de leurs tâches.' Luc Boltanski and Eve Chiapello, op. cit., note 6, pp. 127-128.

13 See Antonio Negri and Michael Hardt, *Empire*, Cambridge University Press, Cambridge 2000.

I speak on behalf of myself

Chris Dercon

In 1995 I was invited by the Berenschot research firm to formulate my thoughts about the coming century on the occasion of the symposium 'De agenda voor de volgende eeuw' ('The agenda for the next century'). The title of my lecture was 'En masse naar Mars?' ('En masse to Mars?').[1] I asked whether we would still find images in our cities, museums and exhibitions that would be adequate, that would bear a certain relevance to our civilization. For, I continued, if we look at the stream of research reports, recommendations, policy documents and official speeches, it is clear that their authors, without a shred of embarrassment, concede that a kind of middle-of-the-road culture (a harsh cultural pragmatism as well as an objectified cultural indifference) will soon be unavoidable. I ended with a creed – my creed for the coming century: 'We should not have to travel to Mars or Saturn for images that match what is deep within ourselves. We must not be satisfied with a purely pragmatic approach to culture, in which the supply meets the supposed demand of the "culture consumer", but instead create a climate in which visual art is alive, undermines preconceptions, evokes longings, makes "the other" within ourselves visible. Makers as well as viewers, transmitters as well as receivers must retake possession of culture. There is no room for indifference in that; it requires a choice. Dare to choose. He who dares not stand up for a personal opinion he can support by arguments, be it at the cost of popularity or income, is no democrat, but a bungler.'

The start of the new century brought stormy weather, not just a middle-of-the-road culture but 'respectable' populism as well. I, however, had made a personal choice and I had to stand up for it. From Rotterdam I called for an intellectual museum, less peaceable art in public space, for cultural tactics of contestation, for outsider art, and for a true emancipation of the viewer. And I expressed my amazement at the tame reactions from the cultural domain to the rise of the populist politician Pim Fortuyn.

In lectures, essays and open letters in newspapers, magazines and specialized publications I tried, publicly, to formulate a critical alternative to a cultural environment that was increasingly dominated by the demands of 'the audience'.[2] At the beginning of my tenure as director of the Museum

Boijmans Van Beuningen, Paul Depondt, in *de Volkskrant*, coaxed the following statement from me: 'distrust the audience'. This pronouncement was widely perceived as negative, even though I had in fact specified in the same interview that since the middle of the nineteenth century the composition of the audience has been in constant flux and with each of these increasingly rapid changes all these different audiences had had different desires and different demands. This alone should be reason enough for distrust when the term 'audience' is used. In Rotterdam, however, it was loud and clear: 'The audience is always right.'

In Rotterdam and the rest of the Netherlands just after the turn of this century, I found less and less of what I had encountered there in the first half of the 1990s: a great curiosity about foreign cultural contributions and 'other' cultural opinions and about their permeability and exchange; concepts that had been defining characteristics of Dutch culture for a very long time were steadily losing significance. The gaze was more and more being turned inward, and it was increasingly difficult to find allies in one's own circle who would openly take a critical attitude toward the populist revival.

Hand in hand with a pragmatic attitude toward life, undeniably strongly developed in the Netherlands – including where culture is concerned – a brazen form of anti-intellectualism began to emerge more frequently and more openly. All of this reminded me in many aspects of the widespread acceptance of the Berlusconi culture.

Was I yearning for the Netherlands of 10 years ago, where not only this great curiosity and demand for exchange was evident, but the compulsion for consensus and conflict avoidance, which I had so feared and despised, reigned as well? I do not think so. Striving for consensus is hardly compatible with being the director of an art museum. For, since the Renaissance, the 'individual interpretation', yes, the doctrine of difference, forms the very point of departure for the creation of autonomous art and along with it the foundation of our art collections. We have to rediscover and play upon all these different, individual interpretations over and over in our museums. Most of us visit museums in order to figure out who we are. And we do this by examining whether our own interpretations match those of others, artists of the past and present, for instance. In my view, the place and role of the museum in society cannot be defined as the sum of the wishes of individual art consumers, but as society's need for a collective cultural space.

The museum as we know it has been in constant flux since its founding, about 250 years ago. It has been seeking its roots and reason for being from the start. And what were we supposed to call this thing that came to be called a museum: treasury, symbol of the nation, archive? What do we do, and especially, what do we exclude? The concept of exclusion weighed and continues to weigh heavily in the founding of museums for modern and contemporary art. Today we are being asked to focus on the reverse of this exclusionary concept, and this is an approach that requires a different way of thinking. The debate now raging about 'high' and 'low' culture is merely an alibi. The first task of the museums is to revisit part of the historical work. And we should especially ask ourselves whether we ought not work in very diverse ways and with very diverse people on the museum as a true instrument of learning, a centre of knowledge and a centre of consciousness in the hands of many.

The museum, as we know it today is hardly a place for knowledge but for mere experiences. The role of the intellectual as the beating hart of the museum seems doomed. Yet this depends on how we define the role of intellectual work in our museums. The enterprise of theory, theory as a theatre of thought, need not solely lead to the consideration of the contemporary or historical references of a work of art. The real challenge lies in creating new forms of representation, emphasizing the other side of meaning. This is never the artwork in itself, but rather something that can be recognized in its effect, in its capacity to liberate the viewer. It is interesting that in this way we can also grant the viewer an increasing level of autonomy. Or to put it more precisely: we allow the viewer a greater level of autonomy than the (relative) autonomy of the artwork.

Most museums, however, do not offer such an exciting, indeed theoretical, context. The Utopia (or democracy) has had to make way for a modest ideal: instead of offering cultural opportunities, we provide cultural services.

Only a few decades ago, practice and theory still seemed to proceed in a never-ending *pas de deux*. This was due, first of all, as rightly observed by the art historian Jeroen Boomgaard[3], to the fact that artists themselves wanted to elevate and shake up the cultural condition of their work. The museum itself is a cultural condition. And the museum and the museum audience must still be won over. That is why we cannot ignore the 'aesthetic history of art exhibitions' (Thierry de Duve). This history has particular bearing on the capacity to judge, the right to cast a vote. This right is a founding principle not only of our democracies, but also of our museums. We must therefore

make possible situations in which many people have an
opportunity to say: 'this is an important part; it belongs in our
culture'. The intellectual museum would be crucial to this
process! For this is also a question of accessibility. In fact, it is
is a necessity, at least as long as we do not define accessibility
solely as 'gaining access'.

Middle-of-the-road culture and 'respectable' populism as
we know them today reject an intellectual attitude. Indeed, one
never speaks on one's own behalf but on behalf of others one
hardly knows, if at all. In today's world, however, an individual
standpoint is more needed than ever.

The 'gate-keepers' in Dutch museum culture – the
directors, administrators and curators – should, instead of
adopting a detached attitude, learn once more how to tell great
and personal stories. Once the fear of one's own gate gains the
upper hand, Dutch culture will become a monoculture, a climate
in which the certainties of peace and order reign but the uncertainties of permeability and engagement stand no chance.

Note

1   M. Metze, O. van Munster (eds.), *De Agenda voor De Volgende
    Eeuw. Het Berenschot Symposium 1995,* Utrecht 1996.

2   'Museum in crisis', *Bulletin Stedelijk Museum Amsterdam*, no. 1,
    2003, pp. 14-21; 'Brief van een museumdirecteur', *De gids*, no. 10,
    October 2001, pp. 812-814 (response to an open letter by Kees van
    Twist, director of the Groninger Museum); 'Abuse of the public
    space', *Archis* no. 5, 2001, pp. 31-36; 'Preface', exh. cat. *Madness.*
    Galerie Atelier Herenplaats & TENT., Rotterdam, 2001, pp. 7-9; 'Der
    Dämon und wie er über die Welt kam. Zum Tod von Pim Fortuyn:
    Wahre Kultur darf nicht auf Angst, Nostalgie oder dunklen Instinkten
    beruhen', *Süddeutsche Zeitung*, 8/9 May 2002, p. 9.

3   Jeroen Boomgaard, 'New communication, No message', *A-Prior* 3/4,
    Brussels 2000.

The platform
of commitment

Jeroen Boomgaard

'We are the world' was the title of the group exhibition in the Netherlands pavilion at the 2003 Biennale in Venice, and there is no better way to describe present-day commitment in art. The works that were shown there formed a perfect summing up of what commitment has given the world in the last few years. The exhibition adopted the multicultural face that the culture of the Netherlands had so deliberately sought, while at the same time it combined the extremes of social commitment in one space with the work of Jeanne van Heeswijk and Alicia Framis. But the title, with all its irony, was above all so effective because it shows the vagueness associated with the notion of commitment at the moment. As Lex ter Braak, director of the Netherlands Foundation for Fine Arts, Design and Architecture, put it at a symposium on new commitment: 'All art is committed, because artists concern themselves with the world'.[1] Commitment has become so general in form and content that it lends itself without any difficulty to a prestigious existence in the official arts circuit, as could be seen in other pavilions as well. This is remarkable since commitment and bodies like the traditional museum have not always got along together.

The museum is often regarded as an obstacle in the contact between art and the world. While the work wants to engage with reality, the museum classifies this endeavour in advance as image. The involvement with the world can be shown in the museum, but it inevitably remains ineffective. That is why avant-garde artists display an aversion to established institutions that goes hand in hand with the search for other platforms for their art. Whether we are talking about the avant-garde of the 1910s and 1920s, that of the 1960s and 1970s, or the latest wave of the 1990s, each time the same idea pops up: the museum has to be destroyed, avoided or radically changed. But it is a good deal easier to identify the scapegoat than the site where it is all supposed to happen. We can imagine a lot in connection with terms like 'the street', 'life', 'everyday reality', but very specific they are not.

The attempt to escape being encapsulated by the space of the museum and the desire to share the fate of genuine life are thwarted by the realisation that art entails the museum. Precisely because the museum is the place par excellence where random products can be recognized as art, those products can only continue to fulfil their function as works of art provided they are set within the golden frame of the museum. So the striving for commitment is often accompanied by an erosion of the parameters of art. Utility and necessity seem to come better into their own once the accursed label 'work of art' has been removed. It is possible to indicate a number of points in history when art tried to link itself in this way with the world. This is not the place for a full historical treatment, but it is worthwhile to consider a few of these moments. The 1960s and 1970s play a crucial role in this respect. We recall them as the years when terms like communication and interaction made their début, but the 1960s also seem to have been the period rather than any other that has consciously or unconsciously served as a model for artists of the 1990s.

A group of artists who already in the mid-1950s wanted to replace existing forms of art by political and socio-political analysis and working for a better society was the Situationniste Internationale. The involvement of the Situationists with the world knew no limits: no less than the total revolutionising of everyday life was on the agenda, and art, even in its avant-garde variant, was regarded as a thing of the past. It is therefore curious that there were plans for an exhibition of the group in the Stedelijk Museum in Amsterdam in 1960. A closer examination of the proposals, however, shows that the commitment was supposed to emerge from a playing off of the museum against real life. A labyrinth was planned in the Stedelijk where the visitor could wander around in spaces with different atmospheric conditions. Narrow, long spaces alternated with high ones, rain, wind and mist, everything was possible. To underline the disruption of the spaces of the museum, the access to the whole would be through a (fake) hole in the outside wall. During their trip through the labyrinth, visitors would hear tape recordings of Situationist conferences. At the same time, however, a *dérive* was planned in the city: members of the Situationist Group would wander through the city looking for remnants of authentic existence, in permanent contact with a central post manned by Constant. While visitors to the exhibition were undergoing a fake experience, they would be made aware of the fact not only by the emphatic Situationist commentary, but also by the event outside from which they were excluded.

It is hardly surprising that the project was cancelled. It might even be surmised that calling it off was a part of the strategy.[2] Although the work of this group is immensely popular at the moment and the word *dérive* crops up all over the place,

it is worthwhile to note the difference from today's compulsion
to participate. For the Situationists, there was no suggestion
that by taking part people would arrive at a better life, gain
insight, or find any other kind of satisfaction. The actions were
intended solely to prepare for or explore a future society, and
total revolution was the condition of its coming into being.
Since art could not play a role of any significance in the status
quo, there was no way of presenting the actions as if it could.
Even so, action needs a platform too, so the Situationists chose
the word to prevent it from disappearing without a trace. The
spoken or printed word was the appropriate medium for avoiding the society of spectacle and at the same time disseminating
the absolute analysis.

Commitment in art came to an end for a time in the late
1970s. One of the last projects clearly shows how large the
dilemmas had become. At the invitation of De Appel in Amsterdam, in 1978 the French artist Hervé Fischer organized a project
within the framework of his Art Sociologique. In those years
the idea of a world revolution had already shifted somewhat
into the local neighbourhoods. Fischer proposed letting the
residents of a particular neighbourhood fill a page in a newspaper themselves. He preferred a problem neighbourhood, like
the Bijlmer in South-East Amsterdam, but both De Appel and
the newspaper involved, *Het Parool*, though each for reasons of
its own, wanted the project to take place in the Jordaan district
in the centre of Amsterdam. Although in the end the page was
filled for a whole week with small pieces written by local residents, the project suffered severely from internal contradic-
tions, such as the way in which words were put into people's
mouths or the role of art. Although one of the aims of the project
was 'to let the people speak for themselves' and to reinforce
their sense of dignity or identity, a lot of preliminary persuasion
was needed to get them to put pen to paper by themselves, and
desk editors then had to direct the word and the identity clearly
in a certain direction. For instance, criticism of government
bodies was favoured because social change was one of the priorities, while complaints about foreigners (also a permanent
aspect of the 'cosiness' for which Amsterdam is famous) were
excluded as undesirable. To disguise the fact that strings were
being pulled behind the scenes, the organization of the project
was not allowed to mention that it was an art project, and
certainly not that an art institution was behind it. In the meantime photographs of the project were shown in De Appel, so that
the schizophrenia that seems to cling to committed art became
fully visible. For while the artist bade art farewell in order to do

something real on the platform of the world, the result was shown on a different platform, the art institution that had funded the project, with the result that the genuine action became symbolic. There were two different platforms that excluded one another, but that were simultaneously occupied by art.[3] It was no longer possible to disguise the ambivalence of committed art, and artists increasingly saw themselves faced with the choice in those years of capitulating to capitalism or breaking radically with art and going underground.

Although it would require a separate text to fully chart the Postmodern aversion to commitment, a few points can be singled out here. It was above all the principal premises of the politically committed art of the previous decades that had suddenly lost their validity. The belief in authenticity was replaced by the idea of a code, and the notion of direct action and direct involvement was replaced by the realization of the inevitability of mediation. But it is above all the collapse of a coherent view of the future and the belief in radical change that destroyed the foundations of commitment. The ambiguity inherent in a project like fischer's was dissolved by drawing the consequence that art is irrevocably art and that the museum is art's natural habitat. At most art could expose the dominant codes and cultures; it had little to contribute to political or social change.

But let us return to the Netherlands pavilion and examine the international spectrum of commitment that was offered there. At first sight there hardly seems to be any political commitment of the kind described above. Although Alicia Framis has emphatically been concerned with the world for years, and the public space is a prior condition of her work, it still seems to concentrate on the individual encounter. At first she used her own person for that purpose, as in the project *The Dreamkeeper* (1998), in which she kept watch by someone's bed for a night. Her most recent work on a special collection of clothes for demonstrators seems to be related to society at a more general level, but here too the encounter occupies pride of place, for example by the presentation of the line among football supporters who do not know what is going on. Her work is thus a good example of what Nicolas Bourriaud has called 'relational aesthetics'. Contemporary art is about relations between people and precisely because of that, he argues, it is in opposition to the art of the society of spectacle. It is a criticism from within; artists have their feet firmly on the ground, which means that the big revolutionary model or the absolute Utopia has been replaced by the micro-Utopia, because artists realise that direct critical action is based on an illusion of originality, on the assumption of a position outside the world that is no longer tenable, or might even be labelled regressive.[4]

Bourriaud also provides the basis for the dominant notion of commitment: art is a relationship with the other, and thereby the work of art demonstrates a relationship with the world.[5] This definition makes it possible not only to compress the world in the individual, as Framis does, but also to contribute to the world as an individual, as seems to be the case in the work of Jeanne van Heeswijk. She believes with conviction in the potential of art and mainly organizes projects in which she involves not only residents of a particular neighbourhood, but also other artists, designers, etc. Encounter is central to her work as well, which presupposes that communication and exchange can lead to an improvement in the conditions in which people live out their lives. Van Heeswijk's work is barely tangible – the process and the organization of what may come out of it in the course of time actually constitute the product of her artistic effort.[6] An important element in it is the link with the local, with a community that is allowed to speak for itself or charged with identity. Still, no matter how active artists may be, this has little in common with the action around which art centred in the past. A major reason for this difference is the lack of an overarching social perspective to serve as a guideline for action. General notions of communication, interculturality and exchange have come to replace a politically charged vision of the future based on a strict analysis of the dominant abuses. The basis for much committed action in public space is no longer the disruption of the system or the erosion of the structure, but individual contact or interaction with a limited and clearly circumscribed group. The emphasis is on participation in everyday life, not on action that unmasks everyday life and exposes the hypocrisy of power.[7]

This return of commitment can only be grasped if we keep postmodern doubt at the back of our mind. The lack of an overarching perspective, the impossibility of escaping from the world, the awareness of mediation, the choice of small-scale contact instead of large-scale change, are all features that emerged at the same time as postmodernism. The realistic, pragmatic attitude on which it is based also affects the relation with the museum and the art world. While commitment in the past believed that it could only function by turning its back on the museum and slagging the art world, present-day artists recognise their dependence on the institutions that disseminate art.

Artists organize actions, exhibit the results and publish on them in art journals and books without making much of a fuss about it. That does not mean to say that this art has no ideals. On the contrary, this commitment is based on models of communication and interaction, as we have seen. Although artists are aware that they cannot escape from the label of art, that does not stop them from using direct contact to tinker with that label. But it is precisely that ideal of removing distance that renders a clear message impossible. The action can only succeed when it is an end in itself; any more long-term effect would make it a priori subordinate to a determinate meaning that would thwart the interaction.

The tendency to make social interaction itself the theme of art is not just the ambition of artists. Exhibition curators and the cultural departments of all kinds of government bodies have welcomed this new trend in art to approach the neighbourhood or community in a new way, and in doing so they display an unlimited confidence in the potential of public participation. An example of this is the project for the Kanaleneiland district of Utrecht, where Jan van Grunsven and Ineke Bellemakers have set up a socio-cultural enterprise that will take several years. The initiative and the funding come from the Utrecht Local Authority, which envisaged two projects: an investigation of whether art could contribute to the socio-cultural context of the district, followed by a second to give the residents in the district more confidence in the future of their locality. It was evident to Van Grunsven and Bellemakers that this was not just another art project, but that it must make an impact on the socio-cultural context of the district. So once again we are talking about a process, not a product. All the same, in this case the outcome seems less non-committed. Since during the formulation the artists discovered that the plan for the restructuring of the district, of which the art project was to form a part, was nothing but a vague notion in the heads of a few managers in the Utrecht Local Authority, they decided to take the first step themselves in the direction of a new approach to an actual restructuring. The plan, which consists of a number of stages, the first of which is a project with the primary schools in the district, increasingly tries to involve the residents themselves in order to arrive at the formulation of an integrated approach to the restructuring.[8]

No matter how understandable and refreshing this new commitment may be in its willingness to engage in direct action, a few critical comments are in order. The desire on the part of artists to be more than decorators of everyday life and to link an existence within art to social interaction is completely legitimate, but its legitimation has its price. Artists today can be as light-hearted as they like when it comes to the relation between the different platforms on which they present their art, but they seem to underrate the effects of the platform itself. In the present case that platform is neither the medium nor the site. Both of those elements came to be regarded as equals in present-day culture some time ago: anything can be art, and art can appear anywhere. The frame and backdrop are determined nowadays much more strongly than before by the rules, descriptions, objectives and justifications that go along with projects of this kind. As a result, the field of play of art is demarcated in a way that tries in advance to rule out surprise or ambiguity, and that for that very reason can only bring about a dubious effect. Hervé Fischer's newspaper project was already determined to some extent by the party placing the commission (De Appel) and the medium (*Het Parool*), but in the case of Framis' *Dreamkeeper* project too, the influence of the institution was greater than appears at first sight: candidates who wanted to have Framis beside their bed were not only actively recruited but also carefully screened.[9] That form of control is present in the background more than ever in social projects in public space that are carried out by the artists involved and commissioned by the local authorities. Of course, there is cooperation with the residents on the spot, and of course the policy of the local authority is raised for discussion, but the question of exactly what government bodies have in mind when they initiate this kind of large-scale and expensive project is not raised. I am afraid that the answer has to be sought in the symbolic content of the art projects. The local authority provides the platform on which the art can be shown, and even if the artist claims that direct action and interaction will be the result of his or her work, in the end it is merely a social process that is performed, a game that is played, and one that by definition will fail to have any consequences. Managers are very pleased with projects of this kind: they confer on them an aura of dedication and involvement without their having to do much for or about it.

The socially committed art of the present betrays a strong predilection for the game. Jeanne van Heeswijk enabled visitors to the Netherlands pavilion in Venice to take part in a children's game of marking out territories. Other projects assigned a major role to working with children. This is not only the return of Huizinga's *homo ludens*, who was also important to the Situationists, but it is also an attempt to forget about the platform by addressing a group for whom the notion of art does not yet have any meaning. Direct action and actual contact are only possible when fixed notions and imposed frameworks are lifted, if only for a moment. For the artist that is a condition of being able to do something that can produce an effect again, while for the government that funds such an enterprise very different interests are at stake. To flesh out the symbolic content, and at the same time to underline the seriousness of the enterprise, without forgetting the legitimation of the amount of money and energy that is put into it, a project of this kind cannot tolerate any ambiguity at all. Precisely because the function of the enterprise is difficult to pin down, because its outcome threatens to be ambivalent, to say the least, every doubt is removed in advance by means of explanations, information brochures and other media by which the consensus society tries to keep itself going. *Homo ludens* is not awakened to lead life in a radically different way, but to play along in the big game of bogus responsibility that we all play.

The committed art of the present suffers from the lack of ambivalence. There has been a growing tendency in the large exhibitions of the last few years to explain works whose content or provenance indicate an involvement with the world in such a way that hardly anything is left unaccounted for. However subtle a work of art may be, the big machinery of institutions, curators and the government, which wants to use art to stage its own involvement with the world, will not tolerate any confusion and strictly rules out any possibility of different layers of meaning. Thus in the history of committed art, text has moved from the artist to the target group to end up with the party placing the commission and the government. Involvement has become a set of regulations.

The Netherlands pavilion also presented a work by Erik van Lieshout. His film *Respect* was shown in a rickety wooden shed filled with Rietveld cinema chairs. Although this film is clearly about the world because it is set in the neighbourhood where Van Lieshout lives among a majority of immigrants, visitors were only too aware of the fact that Van Lieshout had dragged them into an art project. But that is precisely why this work could say more about the way in which art can show a concern for the world than the works that so openly wear their commitment on their shoulder. Art should be concerned about the world, but artists must continue to create their own platform and not allow themselves to become string puppets in the official commitment show.

Notes

1   Symposium in Smart Project Space, Amsterdam, 23 March 2003.
2   'Die Welt als Labyrinth', *Internationale Situationniste*, no. 4, June 1960, pp. 5-7. See also Roberto Ohrt, *Phantom Avantgarde*, Hamburg 1990, and Thomas Y. Levin, 'Geopolitics of Hibernation. The Drift of Situationist Urbanism', in: Libero Andreotti and Xavier Costa (eds), *Situationist Art, Politics, Urbanism*, Barcelona 1996, pp. 111-139.
3   Jeroen Boomgaard, 'De utopie van de argeloosheid. Een korte cursus engagement', *De Witte Raaf*, no. 77, Jan.-Feb. 1999, pp. 23-25.
4   Nicolas Bourriaud, *Relational Aesthetics, les presses du réel*, Dijon 2002, pp. 28-31.
5   Ibid., p. 85.
6   Mirjam Westen, 'Jeanne van Heeswijk: The Artist as Versatile Infiltrator of Public Space: "Urban Curating" in the 21st Century', *N Paradoxa*, vol. 12 (2003), pp. 24-32.
7   For the rise of committed art in the USA see Miwon Kwon, *One Place after Another*, Cambridge (Mass.)/London 2002, esp. Chapter 4: 'From site to community in new genre public art: the case of "Culture in Action"', pp. 100-137. Incidentally, the ambitions and pretensions are often just as grandiose and directly recall those of the 1970s, although that period is not explicitly mentioned. For instance, Jane Jacob, one of the artists involved in the *Culture in Action* project, put it like this: 'In the 1990's the role of public art has shifted from that of renewing the physical environment to that of improving society, from promoting aesthetic quality to contributing to the quality of life, from enriching lives to saving lives' (Kwon, p. 111).
8   Jan van Grunsven and Ineke Bellemakers, *Verkenningsopdracht Kanaleneiland-Transwijk / Conceptversie / 1*, Amsterdam, November 2000, and *Voortgangsverslag <re-start>*, Amsterdam, June 2003.
9   Kwon shows how an artist and a specific community are often interlinked in advance in terms of content, so that there is not much scope for their own contribution. For instance, the US artist Renée Green was invited for a project in Chicago with the group with which she would be working, and the nature of the work was practically laid down beforehand. Kwon: 'Which is to say that the matchmaking mediation of the sponsoring institution, inevitably motivated by the presumption of an artist's interests and the anticipation of a particular collaborative project, often reduces, sometimes stereotypes, the identities of the artist *and* the community group' (Kwon, pp. 140-141).

The sober twentieth century

Arjen Mulder

Looking back over one hundred years of contemporary thinking, one is forced to conclude that the period's highly praised and much-read philosophers do not belong in the library of common sense, but in the front ranks of the twentieth century's cabinet of curiosities. Walter Benjamin, Martin Heidegger, Ludwig Wittgenstein, Rudolf Carnap, Georges Bataille, Jean-Paul Sartre, Louis Althusser, Jean-François Lyotard, Gilles Deleuze, Jacques Derrida, Richard Rorty, E.N. Cioran, to name but a few of the best known: only those who have not yet come down from their twentieth-century high could still take them seriously. Or take a look at some visual art of the period. All those avant-gardes with their celebrated names and despotic leaders – futurism, dadaism, constructivism, surrealism, cobra, pop art, op art, minimal art, conceptual art, postmodernism – you look at it in amazement in the museums of modern art. What on earth did people ever think to see in it? Just how stoned was the art scene during the last hundred years? Or take the political movements with names as outdated as they are impressive – liberalism, communism, social democracy, fascism, Nazism, right, left, progressive, Third Way, free market, plus all their variants and subspecies: you have to have a screw loose to understand what they were all about. And what to think of Schoenberg's replacement of classical harmony with twelve-tone music? Or modernist, not to mention postmodernist, architecture? We have all fallen through the twentieth century and what are we supposed to do now? Start afresh? But that was precisely where twentieth-century people went so badly wrong: in their desire to break with tradition and to start an authentic life of their own, they were an easy target for every fool who claimed to have thought up something radically new.

This is only what I think in the privacy of a tormented, gasping soul. Every century has a genius and the genius of the twentieth was its capacity for destruction. Everything had to be broken so that afterwards it could be put together again in a wholly original way. You can't really blame anyone, not even the Nazis, who spent their formative years as boys of fifteen to twenty among the rotting corpses in the trenches of the Great War and who sometimes saw ten thousand fellow men die in a single day on the orders of the representatives of a previous century.

What is astonishing about the twentieth century is not the devastation and the now gruesome, now clumsy and occasionally tragic attempts to produce something different, something less awful, or at a pinch healthier or fresher or finer; what is astonishing is that in spite of everything, a few people managed to keep a cool head and calmly take the next step in the process in which humanity has been engaged for thousands of years – trying to fathom itself and its purpose in the universe. And the end of the project of humanity is nowhere in sight, however much twentieth-century people may have longed for it and done their best to get to the end of it once and for all. That someone like Einstein should have advised the president of the United States to build an atom bomb… And the ensuing arms race in which hardworking scientists developed one murderous idea after another as if it were a new shampoo or hair gel… Or take the introduction of the automobile which resulted in landscapes all over the world being dug up, bulldozed, hacked to pieces, buried, and that's without even mentioning the air pollution… And all the while, the intellectuals were in a Valhalla or nirvana filled with vacuous ideas that offered no explanation, let alone solution, for the world's problems, but were instead a symptom of them. Start afresh again? Even if one wanted to, it is no longer possible. The best new idea of the last ten, fifteen years is that of restoration – restoration of the landscape, of nature, restoration of the political order, the East Bloc, restoration of the atmosphere, restoration of the economy… A much more revolutionary idea than that of progress nowadays is the idea of going back. Sad, really.

This is what I sometimes ponder in the quiet of an evening suffused with the red of the setting sun. The opposite of normality is not authenticity, originality or singularity. The opposite of normality is terror. The reason ordinary people prefer to live in a highly ordered society is because they get quite enough craziness and disorder in their daily lives. Three feeds a night, tiny teeth breaking through, the whole array of childhood illnesses meaning sleepless nights for mummy and daddy, risky waterside games, the nasty Miss or stupid boy at school about whom parents' committees, school heads and counsellors must be consulted, the Thursday morning swimming lessons, riding lessons, judo on Saturday, football (not just taking and fetching but staying to watch), the neglected pets that still have to be looked after by someone, the gothic garbing of the teenage body plus a room and noise level to match, the endless arguments at mealtimes, the first evenings out while mum and dad bite their nails on the sofa, the souped-up moped, the much too old friend, the summer camps, first holidays with friends in an old van through Europe, the laptop required by schools, the departed lover and all the heartache that entails, the shaky marriage, one's own body that is slowly but surely falling apart, and so on and so forth: every parent who is concerned about their own offspring longs for normality as they long for the tepid bath that brings at least one hour of quiet on a Saturday evening. Authenticity, originality, genuineness are the wrong criteria. With a little thought you soon realize that those concepts defy precise definition. To experience infinity in an intimate circle, in the course of a few years to appreciate what eternity is, to know you are part of a process that is greater that all possible connections between the parts – to experience the existence of the world as an objective mystery, the existence of life as a mystery squared, and then to confront the even greater mystery: that the world and life became conscious of themselves in us. As the carrier of that consciousness, it is incumbent upon humanity to develop all the symbolic, artificial and technical means to broaden, deepen and intensify that consciousness – and then to wait and see how life and the world will answer. And occasionally to kneel and thank Goodness-Only-Knows-Who for these wonders. Terror is all that stands in the way of this.

It is our fate to have the twentieth century behind us. It doesn't have to be repudiated in its entirety, but nor is there any cause to wax nostalgic for the period before its dawning. If you are in the habit of walking around the area where you live, you discover the existence of all sorts of sub-systems: a certain house connects up with a plantation there and with a street a little further along, with a row of houses along an avenue, a building of obscure purpose much further away and perhaps even with an entire neighbourhood, street plan and all. It is not because of their use or the particular point in time when they were built or the architect who was involved in their construction that they belong together: the connection is you – you have discerned the link between them, intuitively, trusting blindly to instinct. You see those parts withdraw from the binding relationship that every city imposes on what and whoever is part of it. They absorb you into their own little world. A city is a myriad of sub-systems, each of which stands for certain feelings, for some-thing that can be registered and experienced, but is not so easily put into words. Some of those feelings you reject (you avoid those areas of the city), others you deliberately seek out.

That's how I see the twentieth century. You can decide for yourself which feelings are productive and which are disabling, which are totally honest and which false or sentimental, which enrich and which obstruct. The twentieth century is an archive from which, with a modicum of thought and energy, whole complexes of people, incidents, political changes, books, encounters, films and photos, entire philosophies even, can be extracted that symbolize, strengthen and enrich precisely those feelings that will take you further. As Dürer remarked about art: 'it's embedded in nature and you only have to extract it, but once extracted it ceases to be nature'. Find the politics, music, art, philosophy which came into being in the thick of the twentieth century but were not affected by it, or only partly, and which consequently lend themselves to further use in humanity's project. From those parts of what is not a whole, build the symbols of your soul – with a bit of luck the genius of the present century, the twenty-first, will emerge from it. They exist, those independent minds who saw their own time as part of a long history rather than as a permanent now. They really do exist. You'll come across them as a matter of course if you look around with a little perseverance, a little *Wanderlust*. There also exists a sober twentieth century.

Always at a distance

Beyond the boundaries of engagement

New commitment

Reflect #01

On 11 September, 2001, the writer Jay McInerney woke up at eight fifteen in the morning. He continued to lie there, and dozed off again until it was twenty to nine. Then he got up and tried to open the blinds – that was difficult as the chain was stuck. When he looked outside five minutes later, he saw smoke rising from the north tower of the World Trade Center, directly in front of his window.

Events from that moment on are well known. At 8.46 am local time, Flight 11 from American Airlines with 92 people on board rammed into the north tower of the WTC. The aeroplane exploded and carved out a hole in the building. Seventeen minutes later United Airlines Flight 175 with 65 people on board flew into the south tower. Both buildings burst into flames. The panic was immense. People tried desperately to escape the buildings, some even jumping, in utter confusion, from windows umpteen storeys high. On television, live, we saw their bodies speeding downwards through space.

At that point Jay McInerney was not an artist anymore. In the English newspaper *The Observer* he describes what he did later – the first few hours after the attack. He phoned his ex-wife and children. He phoned friends. He went out on the street, talking to total strangers. Giving those same strangers his address in case they were unable to find a place to sleep. Stocking up on shopping. So it was some hours before McInerney realised – others had to draw his attention to it – that the twin towers were also used to decorate the cover of his breakthrough novel *Bright Lights, Big City*. Only then did it slowly sink in that the towers were not only office buildings, shells of work and ambition, but also, more importantly, symbols – of capitalism, growth and self-proclaimed freedom. 'It had become something of an iconic image. Now it would have a grim new significance.' But even for a hip writer like McInerney a disaster is not the moment to give reality an extra undertone.

However, that does not apply to everyone. Within a week the German composer, Karlheinz Stockhausen, at a press conference got down to the business of stating that the attack on the WTC was 'the greatest work of art imaginable for the whole cosmos. By comparison we composers are nothing. Artists too sometimes try to go beyond the limits of what is feasible and conceivable, so that we wake up, so that we open ourselves to another world.' Also, the British *enfant terrible* of the art world, Damien Hirst, was quick to describe the attacks as an 'astounding work of art', while the Italian director Dario Fo stated: 'So what is 20,000 dead in New York? Regardless of who carried out the massacre, this violence is the legitimate daughter of the culture of violence, hunger and inhumane exploitation.' The response to these provocations was remarkable: silence. Where such controversial opinions are usually good for some heated discussions, now, after the report in the newspapers, they are dismissed with a shrug of the shoulders. Only a few of Stockhausen's concerts were cancelled, but at this point the composer of *Helikopter-Streichquartett* humbly offered his apologies. The world could not have cared less.

For many artists the first creative outpourings after 9/11 must have been a painful moment. Some must have felt ashamed for the professional distortions of their colleagues, but few appeared to realise that these artistic footnotes said a painful lot about the role of art in the modern world. In recent years, especially in the art world, there has been much talk about art 'pushing the boundaries'. This mainly relates to artists who work outside the museum and gallery circuit and enter the 'real' world – making art in supermarkets, keeping watch over people's dreams at their homes, or cooking noodles for passers-by. However, if the WTC attacks made one point clear, it is the fact that the art world and the everyday world, despite all the good intentions, are still completely separate. Art is, and remains, a free state in which other laws apply than in normal life. This has immense, fundamental advantages for art – because of this free role art is free to play around with social codes and provide effective 'distorted' reflections on everyday life. This division also ensures that artistic codes in 'real life' are accepted, even if artists do things that people in normal life find repugnant or unacceptable. This is a fine prerogative, but for that artists pay a price. Whatever they do, it always remains a comment from an outsider. Their work never comes completely together with real life.

However, there is a boundary line, and that is reached at the moment when art concerns itself with mores that are controversial in real life. Then, in the eyes of society, an artist can go too far – precisely the reason why this boundary line exerts an irresistible appeal over many artists. There are plenty examples of this in recent years, just in the Netherlands alone. For instance, Joep van Lieshout showed a short film at the Fons Welters Gallery in Amsterdam in which several extracts from scat-sex videos were edited together and in which, to the indig-

nation of several critics, turds landed in mouths and diarrhoea
splattered the camera. In Amsterdam's De Praktijk Gallery,
Zoot & Genant staged a performance in which they had sex
every 90 minutes, live on the internet, while for years painter
Ronald Ophuis has made a sport out of pushing the boundaries
of decency. Among other things, he has painted concentration
camp victims raping a woman, a group of footballers ramming
a coke bottle into another player's rear, and two adults over-
powering two small children.

Scat sex, live sex, concentration camps, paedophilia – these
are all socially taboo subjects, or at least come very close to it.
This is the reason such themes form an excellent target for
artists exploring the boundary line between art and society –
what is an added attraction since they serve two artistic objectives at the same time. In the first place, with this kind of work
an artist is categorically referring to the traditional artist's role
of holding up a mirror to society and its conduct. It is not for
nothing that Ophuis always defends his paintings with the
argument that 'if they create a fuss, at least people are thinking
about them'. But that is not the only reason. So-called 'boundary'
art also stresses the individual, free role of art, its function as a
'free state', the function of the art world as a world where
everything is possible – not for nothing can this 'boundary' art
often count on a remarkably benevolent reception. At the same
time most artists realize that simply breaking a taboo is not
enough for overstepping the boundary line. If artists remain
within this, thus they keep to the prevailing social norms, then
their work is accepted without problems. But if artists distance
themselves too much from the norms in real life, they can count
on complete silence. In that case they are so preoccupied with
emphasising their artists' role that the work is considered a
typical artist's outpouring. This applies to Van Lieshout's scat
sex videos, Zoot & Genant's screwing sessions, and it is exactly
what happened to Stockhausen, Hirst and Fo after 9/11.

Yet it is precisely because this boundary line is delicate,
and changes per place and moment, that it remains interesting
for artists to explore. Whatever the case, it is evident that *distance* is also a core concept – both in form and time art greatly
benefits from this. Thus, this far no one has yet succeeded in
making a good artwork about 9/11 – it is too fresh, too close.
Nudity and 'only' sex were guaranteed a hundred years ago to
create a stir, but now in the everyday world they are so normal
that for those in the art world they do not warrant a second
glance. With paedophilia, on the other hand, hardly a problem
thirty years ago, artists nowadays quickly come up against

having their work confiscated, or even face imprisonment.

The most obvious example of 'boundary' art at this time is the holocaust and concentration camps. For years they were taboo subjects, but in recent years have begun to make noticeable inroads in art. Ronald Ophuis is not the only one that likes to incorporate a Nazi victim into his art. A surfeit of examples of this could be seen in the summer of 2002 at the exhibition 'Mirroring Evil' in New York's Jewish Museum. There the Polish artist Zbigniew Libera showed his Lego block constructions of concentration camps, Alan Schecher exhibited a photograph of emaciated men in Buchenwald, in between which he juxtaposed a picture of himself with a tin of *Diet Coke* in his hand, while Tom Sachs showed tins of poisonous gas, printed with brandnames like Chanel, Hermès and Tiffany. That all sounds quite controversial, even vulgar, yet nevertheless reactions to this art were also markedly lukewarm. Twenty years ago these works would have been completely unacceptable – now only small skirmishes and debates occurred. More striking, however, was the obligatory aspect of the skirmishes, like a chess game being set up which after two moves inevitably leads to a draw. When 'Mirroring Evil' opened there were immediate outcries from conservative Jewish organisations. Thereupon the art world pointed to its traditional freedom. Subsequently, Michael Bloomberg, the mayor of New York, took a halfhearted stand, the museum issued a toned down press release and the exhibition simply continued – protests dealt with. For the artists involved it undoubtedly confirmed their role as a seismograph of social changes. But that obligatory aspect certainly said such a lot.

This evoked an important question, which after the events of 9/11 was made even more meaningful: can an artist actually shift artistic boundaries? In order to answer this question properly, it should first be established that art has courted controversy for centuries, and artists in their work have stretched the moral boundaries and taboos of real life for just as long. It is only a question of how far that consciously occurred. While it is tempting to regard every form of avant-garde art as a form of exploring boundaries, that is precisely what it is *not* about. Avant-garde art forms are, by definition, changes that completely take place within the realm of art. The criticism and commotion they cause outside of this, have less to do with the corroding of moral and social boundaries, than with the fact that the new codes of interpretation that such art ushers in have yet to find their place within society – something which invariably occurs with almost every avant-garde form.

Art which wants to declaim these moral boundaries has a

much more limited tradition. At first it did not go beyond
painters or sculptors transgressing public decency in their work.
This in its turn had everything to do with the fact that art, until
well into the nineteenth century, was considered a world which
was not separate from the everyday one, and what is more, was
on a higher and more exalted plane than this. Thus Caravaggio
was chided for his models having dirty feet and later Gustave
Courbet was criticised for his scenes being too mundane.
Remarkable enough, this 'moral sense' extended to works of art
that nowadays we consider controversial for other reasons. A
painting like Goya's *The Third of May 1808*, with the man about
to be executed, is mainly seen now as a human tragedy and a
statement against the horrors of war in general. However, the
spectators who saw that canvas when it was first exhibited by
Goya in 1814 thought quite differently. To them the painting
was largely a propaganda and journalistic statement, campaign-
ing against the ousted French and offering support to the
returning Spanish king, Ferdinand VII – exactly in the same way
photographs of proud Americans or powerless Iraqi are viewed
as examples of journalism today.

This attitude only changed in the nineteenth century with
the arrival of concepts like *L'art pour l'art* and avant-garde in
art. In practice this largely meant that modern art adopted less
of a subservient position towards the 'real' world. From that
point on, art departed from its serving, journalistic and memo-
rising functions and increasingly referred to itself – the dividing
wall between art and society was raised. Art was strengthened
in this attitude because the 'real' world reacted extremely
tolerantly towards this development, with the result that art
and society quickly began to propel each other into a spiral of
tolerance. By the early nineteenth century the dirty feet of
Caravaggio's model had not been a problem for a long time,
although the realistic images of Courbet's simple working folk
were still considered a provocation. However, the spectator
quickly got used to this as well – a signal for art to move on
further, from workers, to whores, to nudes, to explicit sex, mutilation and disfigurement. In this sense, the breakthrough of
abstract art is highly symbolic – it denoted not only a crucial
development in the world of the arts, but also symbolised the
definitive abandonment of art's role as a mirror of society. And
society also accepted that – deeply convinced, almost humbly
bowing to the prerogatives of art. Art thinks.

Only in the 1960s was it apparent that something quite
different had happened. At that moment art had reached a point
where it was at a loose end on how to highlight ever more the

boundary between art and society. Art was a bonfire of freedom in those years, a bonfire of the vanities as well, a world in which everything was possible. Rudolph Schwarzkogler mutilated his own penis, Chris Burden had himself crucified, Marina Abramović did structural self-castigation and the art world thought it splended and saw it as a confirmation of its own freedom. But society, meanwhile, had had enough: it knew the mechanism, saw through it and shrugged its collective shoulders. The term 'repressive tolerance', which the philosopher Herbert Marcuse coined during the period to describe social changes and the reaction of the elite to these, perfectly reflects the situation of the then art of the day. Despite all its controversial messages, this art was not thwarted and so appeared to be accepted. But in essence, that lack of opposition is a sign of indifference. The art world became a world in itself, an unbounded, unrestrained world that forfeited its rights as a seismograph, commentator and mirror of the real world. The boundary wall became too high.

The fatal, but for art, crucial consequence of this mechanism was first made obvious by Arthur C. Danto in 1964. In that year the philosopher visited an Andy Warhol exhibition in New York's Stable Gallery and saw for the first time Warhols *Brillo Boxes*. In its attempt to exert pressure on the boundaries between art and reality, to expand the domain of art as much as possible, here art has created an autonomous reality which corresponds completely with the everyday one – even more so because it is without taboos. For Danto, Warhol's *Brillo Boxes* symbolize this development. He rightly stated that as a spectator of these boxes you could no longer *see* that they were art – and the same can be said for every object you can think of. The real world and the art world have become parallel universes, virtually identical, in which the meaning of an object is only determined by the world in which it finds itself – the real or the art world.

Danto's observation came at a good moment, exactly at the point that art threatened to overlap society, for it was evident that society did not need art any more at all. In society an entirely individual visual culture arose with its own dynamics – that of advertisements, photography and television. These emphatically distinguish themselves from art because they are widely accessible, do not throw up any barriers and, in particular, do not wish to separate themselves at all from the everyday. Television culture is a consumer culture, a culture of the masses, which because of this has every interest to root itself deeply within society. Thus, from the 1950s onwards, when the first televisions appeared, an autonomous culture for providing

meaning arose *within the everyday world.* This provides an
immense stimulus to the way in which people are aware of
interpretation and visual culture. They have become increasingly
convinced of the fact that the everyday world is not without
ambiguity. They also realize they are manipulated by
advertisements, by looking at television and that even the print
media is not completely objective. At the same time a phenomenon like 'fame' is achievable for everyone – you need only to
appear on television.

It is precisely the mechanism of an autonomous visual
culture that is slowly beginning to also get through to artists.
Through television and the internet, artists who want to over-
step the boundary line between art and society are forced to
abandon the seclusion of the art world in order to function in
the everyday one. And making controversial, cutting-edge art
would seem to be just the thing. Artists who venture to do this
kill three birds with one stone. Regarding content, they can
again refer to their roles as 'explorers' of the boundaries between
art and real life. Moreover, they finally reach a wide audience
with their work and thereby regain their 'social relevance' and
lastly, in so doing, they also achieve the status of the celebrities
of the television age – the actors, presenters and pop stars.

This three-stage mechanism means that modern artists
are more than willing to generate publicity – and at the same
time find themselves manoeuvred into an impossible position.
Because artists who consciously erode the boundary between
art and society, via the mass media, cannot automatically refer
to the artistic tradition. The artist who really wants to enter
the big world also has to work according to the rules of that real
world – and is therefore no longer an artist. If there is one thing
television, film and advertisements have got through to the
general public it is that getting noticed, or drawing attention in
some way, does not serve merely noble artistic goals, but works
particularly well for those that want to be (temporary) ahead of
the rat race of real life. It is not for nothing that it is mainly
television celebrities and ad agencies that make abundant use
of the mechanism of 'distinction' (Benetton !). They do not do
that because they want to imitate the strategies once thought
up by the art world – as some art observers in a late rush of
vanity seem to think nowadays – but because pushing boundaries has evolved into a successful marketing tool. Controversy
attracts attention – and sells.

Thus the anti-social stance, the traditional role of the artist
as outsider, was completely eroded when art took its eye off the
ball for a second. Pushing boundaries is now public property

and so any artist venturing an attempt in that direction must
compete with the likes of Oprah Winfrey, Britney Spears and
Osama bin Laden. This makes artists who, despite this development, still refer to the old boundary line between art and society
immensely naïve – and this naivety disqualifies them as interesting artists. People like Ophuis, Zoot & Genant, and Van Lieshout (in the case of his scat-sex video) are like old, dilapidated
comics who after many decades bang on the door of their old
theatre and expect everyone will automatically stand up and
cheer them. Artists continue to suggest that they want to 'confront' things, 'expose' things, while they should realise, should
be even deeply convinced, that the public has not needed them
in that sense for a long time.

Furthermore, the general public knows full well that
artists like Ophuis, who purports to want to make people think
about horror, are not genuine. Anyone who really feels the horror
of Birkenau would not dream of using their imagination for
this, which does not take them beyond showing or describing.
This is precisely what Theodor Adorno meant when he wrote in
his essay *Cultural Criticism and Society* (1951) that 'After
Auschwitz, to write a poem is barbaric'. What applied then, and
still applies now, is that art which wants to maintain itself must
want to be an outsider, and therefore accepts the consequences
that its comments are not always relevant. This is apparent
from reactions by artists who were involved in 9/11. Those that
saw the towers collapsing – Jay McInerney, Amitavh Ghosh or
Brett Easton Ellis – had no need for ambiguity or controversy.
They limited themselves to writing reports, journalistic items
or impressions. The artistic 'take' came from artists who witnessed the attacks thousands of miles away on television. The
detached remarks by Stockhausen, Hirst and Fo had to be a
reminder of the artistic and independent view an artist has on
the world, but confirmed what increasingly more people think –
that artists are not really engaged in real life.

And this is it, of course. The best artists, who are really
actively concerned about their art and society, are on the sidelines. This was also the major power behind the best works at
the recent 'Documenta': they were engaged, showed things
without demanding a role in the everyday world. The very best
example of this was the film *Western Deep* (2002) by Steve
McQueen in which he showed the fate of a group of South
African goldminers. The film is like a message from the under-
world. McQueen begins with just under ten minutes of darkness
in which we only hear a lift descending into the mine shaft. The
images that follow are no more than impressions of the daily

work – not documentary ones, but images and short sequences, so unusual, but grippingly edited, that more than half the spectators who entered the gallery with me were unable to watch the entire film.

Something similar applies to one of the best artworks made in the Netherlands in recent years, the short film *Bantar Gebang* (2000) by Jeroen de Rijke and Willem de Rooij. Here, too, probably by chance, the backdrop is a harrowing chunk of reality – the Bantar Gebang refuse dump in Indonesia, where hundreds of people live. De Rijke and De Rooij stood facing the dump with their camera, doing little more than filming the sun rising – an extraordinary subtle display of light, colour and small movements. Some critics thought the film, like McQueen's, was too social, too political. But they overlook the fact that in the first place *Bantar Gebang* and *Western Deep* are about form – they are incisive amalgams of colour, rhythm and time and contain associations with the art world and society, whereby the last two aspects are no more important than the first. And their form means these films will never be shown in the cinema or on television – too anti-social. Thus the films *Bantar Gebang* and *Western Deep* (I am convinced photographs, paintings or sculptures would have been just as suitable) are perfect examples of what art achieves when it recognizes its place, when it dares to dissociate itself in order to bombard the world with images, forms and messages from its own den (or rubbish dump in the case of De Rijke and De Rooij). In fact within such a restricted territory, art can find a role again in which it justifies its relationship to society and, more especially, to itself.

What critically engaged artists?

Rutger Pontzen

Looking back it was only a brief period – no longer than a year. Let us say, the time of *Nice!*[1] That art was both engaged and small scale. That the Spanish artist Alicia Framis took up the idea of sleeping alongside complete strangers – in Amsterdam, Luxembourg and New York – keeping watch over the dreams (and nightmares) of others like a white angel. The same time, in the 1990s, when the American Otto Berchem received prospective students at the Rijksakademie with coffee and rolls in his green room, before they were steered to the directorate for an interview. When Française Marie-Ange Guilleminot massaged the feet of tired museum visitors, and the Dutch artist Reneé Kool hired two professional hostesses to greet visitors as they entered an exhibition with the openers: 'Hi, how are you today? You're about to enter an extraordinary show at the Fodor Museum. We do hope you'll enjoy this show.'

While it is not even ten years ago, these projects appear to be from a distant past, since socially engaged art, in the meantime, has again shifted into a higher gear. Small human values have been exchanged for big political ideals, social objectives and criticism of economic developments on a global scale. Art has become more of an activist.

Art and engagement – from an historical perspective, this combination is as old as art itself. Artists have always been involved with what was happening in society. With religious and political issues. In service to kings, bankers and politicians or as independent spirits who could not refrain from reflecting on what was happening in the world. Only this was never labelled 'engaged art'. For centuries it was known as straightforward art. At least I cannot recall having ever read that Michelangelo, Granach the Elder or Jan Steen ever saw themselves as socially engaged artists. Yet this involvement was very much depicted in their paintings, be it the depiction of great biblical themes, the emerging middle class of wealthy burghers or a straight-forward (but morally tinted) St. Nicholas evening.

The engagement lay simply enshrined within the work itself – involvement as a part of the image; the image as an inalienable expression of the artist's involvement. Around 150 years ago changes occurred to this. The arrival of the engaged artist, as a separate type, is a noteworthy and relatively recent phenomenon. And the origin of this can be historically explained.

Not so much through the emergence of this separate type, but through the autonomy of art. In the nineteenth century art became more autonomous. Artists, mainly from the well-to-do classes, had less need of uplifting subject matter (the same as all the other citizens at the time who basked in the optimism of the beginnings of prosperity). What preoccupied them was more the sun setting above London's Houses of Parliament, trains departing from Saint Lazare station in Paris, still-lifes with undefined pomegranates and paintings of a group of friends or colleagues smoking pipes at a café table.

Art was what the eye saw, and what the artist's hand made of that on the canvas. And so modern art was born. Something like this required a response, and this came as well. Possibly through the series of etchings by Francisco de Goya about the horrors of the Napoleonic war in Spain (made around 1815, but only seen for the first time in 1863). In the mid-nineteenth century, visual bourgeois art at the same time acquired its antipode in critical engagement art. And this split has remained since then, no matter how much art has changed over the last century. Even that of critical engagement art – from the peasant farmers of Jean-François Millet and the cartoons of Honoré Daumier, via the German Expressionists and Dada, to Joseph Beuys, the Guerrilla Girls and the small-scale engagement with the human face from the 1990s. And now again large-scale political involvement, namely shown this year in such exhibitions as 'Dreams and Conflicts' (Venice Biennial), 'Attack!' (Kunsthalle, Vienna) and 'Violent Violence' (Arti et Amicitiae, Amsterdam).

Thus, 150 years ago engagement changed into *critical* engagement. The involvement of artists was no longer focused on showing their feeling of solidarity with what was happening in the world, but on depicting the wrongs of it with a view to making possible changes. And as a result, a pressing question arose – how effective is this critical engaged art, in fact? Has it indeed improved the world or made it a fairer place? Is it possible to change anything about the world anyway?

Art and critical engagement – the problem is that this is about two unalike quantities. Two terms that are difficult to reconcile. Critical engagement by definition is aimed at effect. Whether it be about changing a mentality or a goal-oriented action (political, social or economic) that will produce tangible results. It has an objective. Always. That has to be so, otherwise it has no right to exist.

Art is so very different. Art has no objective. It does not have anything in mind. It only knows an effect of evoking, in as far as the spectator is receptive to this. Art *is*, while the critical engaged artist *wants* something. So the term critically engaged art is a contradiction in terms – an inherent contradiction. Critical engagement and art do not tolerate each other. They preclude each other.

The fact that something exists like critically engaged art has less to do with art itself, but more with artists' attitudes. They have something in mind that lies outside the realm of art. It is not the artwork itself that is the centre of their interest, but the involvement with the world and the desire to change something about this. And that intention is now greater than it has ever been. How many exhibitions are there nowadays about the disadvantages of ethnic minorities? About their poor rates of pay, wretched working conditions and the moral repugnance of child labour? Violence on the streets? Wars and people's territorial attitude? These are not exactly the least important subjects under review. Set off against such high ideals, many artworks nowadays are little more than powerless gestures. The goal of really changing these kind of injustices, via art, has not resulted in anything. And this makes art of the 1990s so likeable – it had no objective outside itself. The small-scale aspect of washing feet, welcoming visitors and sleeping with strangers has not really changed society. That was not the intention anyway. The desire was to make the world a more pleasant place. This succeeded for a number of years. But goodness me – that really seems a long time ago.

Note

1   Rutger Pontzen, *Nice! Towards a new form of commitment in art* (Fascinations 9), Nai Publishers, Rotterdam 2000.

The art, the curator and the big clean-up

New commitment

During the press days at the last Venice Biennale, curator Hou Hanrou handed out copies of a *Survival Guide for Demonstrators* to Arsenale visitors: a ragged pink newspaper containing tips for demonstrators that included the best places to demonstrate in the world's big cities, train and bus connections, safety regulations, and the legal rights of people taken into police custody. Hidden amidst all this information was a personal statement made by the Guide's compiler, Jota Castro: 'I like demos. To me they are an art: the flag – Europe Agricola 1 & 2 and Euro trucks. The more alternative, the merrier.' Not exactly a text that reveals a brilliant artistic idea, but the acknowledgements changed everything. There Castro tipped his hat to Hou Hanrou, the Palais de Tokyo in Paris and a major French gallery, instantly transforming a rather superfluous information sheet to a socially engaged work of art – complete with seal of approval.

This expression of engagement was not an isolated incident in Venice. The further you penetrated into the Arsenale, which had been furnished by such heavyweights as Catherine David and Hans-Ulrich Obrist, the more work you saw that suggested a revived political consciousness in art. We saw photographs and video images of runaway urbanization, injustice, poverty and war – in short, portraits of an era that cast a pall of gloom. That gloom became even more intense as it dawned on us that the curators had found nothing to serve as a counterweight. The work was of a documentary nature for the most part, but it was not neutral. Much of it attested to a sense of indignation that was as predictable as it was gratuitous, none of it contributing to any really new vision. There wasn't a single perspective of a better, future world or a visionary analysis of the world we now live in. Obrist must have sensed this lack because he had decided to introduce utopian thinking, but *from the outside*. As a result, his part of the exhibition consisted mainly of *ambience* – and a frivolous political ambience as that from the sixties and seventies.

That ambience was the product of a cluttered sitting and Internet area, a chaos of posters, folders, information stands and public-friendly installations in the garden. Apart from a few works, it produced a feeble form of audience participation and some attempts to copy the political and social defiance of the 60s and 70s without being committed to anything. What we were hearing loud and clear was what we had been suspecting for quite some time: that art badly wants to become socially engaged once more – but it no longer knows how, or with what.

So does this mean art is becoming impotent? That it is no longer capable of formulating what it stands for? What its values are? Or has the time come to ask ourselves whether there isn't something fundamentally wrong with the combination of art and engagement?

Let's go back to the real 70s: to 1 May 1972 to be exact, the date when Joseph Beuys, along with a Korean and an African student, swept up the Karl-Marx Platz in West Berlin with a broom. This 'social action', as the performance was called, had to be understood as a protest against the division of Germany and of the world into a capitalist and a communist camp. But the performance of Beuys 'the Shaman' had another, higher dimension. The sweeping of the square recalled Jesus' driving out the moneychangers from the temple, giving new significance to the heap of swept-up cigarette butts, paper and beer cans. The rubbish became a symbol, an emotionally charged sign of a materialistic form of society in which the public space had been desecrated, the idealistic thinking (of Karl Marx) corrupted and the community divided. The artist's broom swept straight through it all: a symbol of hope and restoration, of bringing together what had been driven apart, and of the reunification of extremes, both in society and in the human soul.

Beuys is dead. He died in 1986, and no one since then has had the courage to take up his idea of the artist as leader and healer. Nor is such a thing possible, for the corruption of this Romantic idea had become fully visible in Beuys's own lifetime. The attributes with which he had fashioned his artistic persona in the early 60s – the survival vest, hat and walking stick – had by the early 80s assumed a different significance. It was a much stronger significance, at least in terms of effect and accessibility. The attributes, along with the grease, felt and copper that he used as materials, were transformed from a personal and at the same time an elevated symbol into a *brand name*, a commercial sign that is part of what you might call 'the strategy of ambiguity': exclusivity combined with maximum distribution. Whether Beuys was fully aware of this commercialization is an open question. He may really not have seen that the media spectacle organized in connection with his fraternal espousal of Warhol closely linked him to Warhol's statement that art is business. Perhaps he thought that the spectacle industry could bring art closer to the outside world without endangering its special qualities.

There's not a single ambitious young artist alive today who is that naive. He (or she) knows all too well that while art has an extraordinary symbolic effect, it also functions as a product that must be 'marketed' – by means of the strategy of ambiguity. Some, such as Kkep and Orgacom, even have names that serve as brands. It's been a long time, moreover, since the exclusivity of the art product was to be found in its uniqueness and authenticity. These concepts were subjected to death by irony during the 80s by artists such as Jeff Koons, Rob Scholte and Sherrie Levine. What more than ever determines the exclusivity – and at the same time the marketing – of a work of art today is the *context* within which it is presented. For a very long time that context was given structure by the guardian of traditional art history, the museum. Today it's become the playground of a phenomenon that we could already see at work in Venice: the 'flying curator'.

In order to properly locate this new phenomenon, we must first examine the notion of context and what kinds of things are linked with it. You might call context a kind of aura, a delicate casing of ideas that transforms the object around which it is wrapped into something more than it actually is. If these ideas reach above or beyond the subjects or personal realities maintained within the social order, then the object is transformed into a spiritualised *symbol*. If they are connected to functional and instrumental conceptual frameworks and strategies, then the object functions as a *code*, a sign for social and economic positions and ambitions.

The symbolic value of art traditionally lies in our search for mystery, for that which is greater than ourselves. The art of the twentieth century no longer links that symbolic value with religion but with the notions and concepts of modernism, the aesthetic theory of modernity that is rooted in Romanticism. This theory is based on an idea that in our time has proven itself an irreconcilable contradiction: the idea of an art that is both autonomous and held up as idealistic and progressive. This duality was a decisive factor in the development of art, the nature of artistic institutions and the direction of artistic discourse. An art emerged that on the one hand formally rendered its autonomy and exaltedness: from now on, the mystery would be hidden in the visual means of expression; and on the other hand linked its idealism to making a conscious break: renewing tradition by rigorously opposing it at every turn. Modernism's anti-traditional movement would become a tradition in itself during the second half of the century.

The museum (by which is meant the museum of modern art) played a central role in this development. It provided the context by keeping watch over the modernist tradition and at the same time by presenting and legitimising the 'anti-traditional tradition'. But the museum has lost this experimental allure in recent decades. It is no longer succeeding in taking on board and accommodating new developments that broaden or question the current notion of art, and it is seen today more as a static institution than as a dynamic one. This means that art has lost both its home and its point of reference, and is now knocking on so many different doors that it's at risk of becoming a free-floating form of *creativity*.

It is true that the problems of the museum are related to the economization of the culture, which compels the museum to contradict itself and to change from a cultural temple to an enterprise like any other, preferably tuned into the entertainment industry. But the museum itself is contributing to its own misery. It defends the autonomy of art with an appeal to higher values that are intrinsic and thus not open to discussion, thereby ignoring the *moral* aspects. At the very most it regards these aspects as abstractions that provide food for the discourse. The paradox is that in doing so the museum places itself on an equal footing with just what it fancies itself to be superior to: the flat world of visual culture. Because the visual culture doesn't immerse itself in the moral aspects of images, either, but releases them worldwide in huge numbers without taking any responsibility for their content or attaching any consequences to their impact. And why take responsibility, if the museum – as representative of the 'higher culture', the culture that sets itself up as the civilization's yardstick – does essentially the same thing?

Fierce protests were already being raised against the one-sided modernist approach three decades ago. The feminist movement, also known as 'the other avant-garde', has been particularly vocal. In the collection of essays containing the important aspects of the feminist discourse from that period, *Framing Feminism, Art and the Women's Movement 1970-1986*, published in 1987, editor Griselda Pollock even describes modernism as 'the hegemonic culture of patriarchal capitalistic societies'. This culture, she thunders, cherishes the idea of the value-free aesthetic gaze. But that idea is a lie, for 'Curators, critics, historians operate within socially specific and ideologically bounded frameworks. What is included, what is omitted, how objects are presented, defined or evaluated, all this is not a reflection of the inherent qualities or meanings but representations of current meanings which therefore are inflected by the inequalities and social hierarchies of the society which is doing the classifying, curating and management of culture.'

An important goal of the feminist cause was reached during the 90s: the 'patriarchal culture' has made plenty of room for female artists and their specific choice of subjects: the body, the personal and emotional life, and gender. And now that every ambitious exhibition organiser makes sure his programme includes a number of non-Western artists, 'Western hegemony' seems to have been penetrated as well. But this is not to say that any substantial change has taken place in the way images are selected and meaning is instilled. A few years ago, the Nigerian artist Oladélé Ajiboyé Bamgboyé, in his book *Writings on Technology and Culture*, published by Witte de With, wrote, 'The histories from other cultures continue to be excluded, as they are often drafted in as exotic plug-ins to the (still) centralized Western canon. (…) Everyone still has to talk the same language of Reason, and as related to the Western context.' What is missing from that context, he then adds, is dialogue.

Bamgboyé is right: the art world does not exchange ideas with other cultures, not at the level of museums and the curators, and only sporadically in the artistic discourse. Not only does such an exchange not exist, but it never could exist, because it would mean giving up the idea that art has a high-minded, intrinsic value, a *universal* value that separates it from details – from cultures and histories that are 'peripheral' because they share little or no common ground with modernism. It is from this claim to universality that art still derives its autonomy, that elevated form of freedom that makes it possible for art to set itself up as a 'sanctuary' outside society and to ignore the fact that it is a part and even a symbol of a specific culture: the culture of 'the free West'.

The 'flying curators' are the missionaries of 'universal' art. They fly around the planet non-stop by plane, e-mail and cell phone, incessantly tracking down artists who can be fit into the discourse. The discourse has become flexible. It no longer follows the gnarled line of tradition and anti-tradition, because that would require the authority of the museum and, as we have seen, such authority has almost no effect. Today's discourse focuses on themes that head curators trot out at the exhibitions they themselves organize.

How and why these themes are chosen is not always clear; the flying curators like to leave the enigmas for the critics to explain. If it's a big, prestigious exhibition such as 'Documenta' or the 'Whitney Biennial', the museum will still resonate with problems having to do with aesthetics and ethics, autonomy and socially focused art. But in general the aesthetic aspect of art is no longer a matter of major importance. And often, as the Venetian 'demonstration news sheet' illustrates, it's not even a matter of minor importance. What counts more than anything else is the context, i.e. the way in which the curator gives form to his moral involvement in big problems – on the basis of art, obviously.

But how engaged is the art itself? Is it really as free and universal as the curator, with his global quest, would have us believe? Often we get the impression that the artist has adjusted his words and even his ideas to suit what he thinks the curator wants.

Let's take a close look at an article that appeared this year in *Archis*[1] on relational art', a contemporary form of engaged art that is being pushed by the head curator of the Palais de Tokyo in Paris, Nicolas Bourriaud.[2] In the words of the author, curator Jens Hoffman, this is art that 'does not limit itself to commenting on society in the form of visual or textual metaphors, but instead creates strong social connections and puts them to work.' One of the examples he gives is the *Velodream* bicycle project made by the Italian Patrick Tuttofuoco for the SMAK in Ghent in 2001. It consisted of ten futuristic bicycles designed and built by Tuttofuoco on which the public were invited to ride around the cycling track of the Ghent velodrome. The movement and the tempo of the riders were accompanied by music by the Milan group BHF.

Sounds like fun. In any case it's an example of art that easily slips into the entertainment culture – but as the artist himself must have realized, rather lacking in substance for an engaged work of art, especially if the curator wants to claim that it is 'deeply involved in the participatory effect of art'. Tuttofuoco found the solution by calling the bicycles 'portraits of intimate friends', thereby giving the work personal surplus value. So Hoffman was able to gratefully write that 'the work metaphorically suggests how his friends take the weight of others onto their own shoulders', and the honour of the socially sensitive art was saved.

But does that honour mean anything anymore in today's social and political life? The surprising thing is that you almost never hear this question being asked in the art world. Conversations are humming with the word 'engagement', and heavy political philosophers such as Antoni Negri and Giorgio Agamben amble through the discourse, but whether this has any influence or is seriously connected in any way to the *real* world is not up for discussion. It's as if the art world as subject matter is nothing but a pretext for keeping the exhibition circuit going, or put in more economic terms, a pretext for the production and distribution of art.

In the collection of essays entitled *Kunst in crisis*[3] (Art in Crisis), philosopher and fashion specialist Guus Beumer expresses amazement that 'despite the price agreements among museums, gallery keepers and artists, despite publicity deals with the media, despite the economic domination of the institutional parties', the artistic discourse has remained purely academic. How is this possible, he wonders. Could it be, he suggests rhetorically, that 'this artistic discourse (...) is no more than a sham, staged for the interests of the market?'

That's a serious suspicion, and difficult to refute. Because if you weigh Hou Hanrou's demonstration news sheet, Obrist's 'utopia' corner and Hoffmann's *Velodream* for their intellectual and social significance, you end up with little more than fantasy – phantoms floating above the concepts whose philosophical depth or social-political expressiveness have been adapted to the artistic discourse. In the hands of the curators, that discourse has become completely ingrown, a cocoon, a closed system of elevated abstractions in which works of art function as codes for 'Idealism', 'Commitment', 'Apocalypse', or whatever the theme of the exhibition might be. In such a context, 'art' is hardly more than a brand name, a product whose intrinsic value is expressed in an ambience: the ambience of rebellion, nostalgia or good intentions that are not to be taken too seriously.

So what now? What is there left for art to do, now that the concepts on which it based its image of itself – autonomy, universality, intrinsic values, sanctuary – have become the components of a *marketing instrument*: the 'discourse of the curators'? This discourse is fighting a mock battle with a culture that would still like to draw distinctions between moral values but no longer knows how. It promotes art as an elevated climate of ideas, but at the same time lays down what those ideas are. Art as code has been robbed of its most precious possession: the freedom to imagine the world and the human individual as potentiality, as something which in a mysterious way always escapes language, images, the general rationalization of life. That freedom was once a symbol of hope for art: hope for restoration, for the unification of extremes, for the good and the beautiful. But why abandon that hope? Artists of the world, pick up your brooms!

Notes

1 Jens Hoffmann, 'On relationships, appropriation and other concerns', *Archis* no. 3, 2003.

2 Nicolas Bourriaud, *Esthétique Relationelle*, Les presses du réel, Paris 1998.

3 *Kunst in crisis*, Prometheus, Amsterdam/ De Vleeshal, Middelburg 2003.

Commitment – what commitment?

Bas Heijne

Dutch intellectuals and artists have been walking around with
a frown for the last few years: they wanted commitment again,
but with what? Since the collapse of the classic political commitment of the artist, art had become alarmingly introverted.
Of course, there were plenty of artists who were not at all concerned, who withdrew into the world of the personal without
any feelings of guilt and threw themselves into exploring the
innermost part of their interior, but many others felt that something was amiss. For them commitment was almost a goal in
itself, an abstract yearning that wanted to find fulfilment in itself.
They wanted to be engaged – it did not matter very much with
what. Forums and discussions were organised on 'the need for
commitment', lectures were given and symposia were held, time
and time again. The outcome was always the same: on the one
hand, the conclusion was drawn that the ideological commitment to which so many twentieth-century artists had been
converted was hopelessly bankrupt and they were accused of
having simply been accomplices in the hero-worship of murderous regimes like that of the Soviet Union; while on the other
hand there was still a longing for the days when art – and the
artist – still mattered in social terms.

Much of this was nothing but egocentric nostalgia, the
common sort of nostalgia for the excitement of the past, when
meaning could be found in bold pronouncements about the
world and heroic deeds. When in a lecture for the NOVIB a
couple of years ago I declared the twentieth-century artist's
political commitment no longer viable, there were vigorous
protests from the auditorium at such cynical arrogance – men
with Palestinian scarves and poking fingers attacked me with
the doggedness of people who are being stripped of a religion.
The myth of the artist's commitment was strong – apparently it
was the good intentions that still mattered, not their catastrophic outcome. But the collapse of the classic political commitment of the artist also generated a real loss – the sunder-
ing of the direct link between the artist and the outside world.
After the débâcle of the political commitment of the sweeping
gesture – what are we doing with China? – there was nothing
left for artists but their own personal experiences and art for
art's sake. That was a lot – but was it enough? Not if you heeded
the constant call for a new commitment, that recurrent longing

for art that meant something in the world, art that directly produced an effect. What made that longing urgent was not just nostalgia, but without doubt also the rise of the global mass culture, with its relentless offensive of images and information and impulses that carry you away. Now that art had retreated from the world, its role in the public domain seemed to have been taken over once and for all by the media, which urged people to become involved with the world around them. The artist as public conscience was replaced by the media star; if a good cause needed defending, it was better to ask a soap star or a pulp fiction writer to do so than an artist. When it was a question of direct commitment, when petitions had to be signed, signatures collected or donations made, it was not opinions and the quality of insights that counted, but primarily popularity; and as far as popularity was concerned, artists did not rate very high in the mass culture.

Two things coincided painfully: the collapse of the artist as moral conscience, and the apparent drop in the importance of art as such. Not only did the figure of the artist hardly play a role in public debate, but art itself seemed to have been driven out to the fringe of society too. It is hardly surprising that the distinction between art and entertainment became more and more blurred.

So you can also regard the attempt to reanimate the political commitment of art as an attempt to restore an important role to art itself. Art does not concern itself with the world from a position of prestige, but from an asking, if not begging position. It asks society to take it seriously again and to allow it to play a significant role in the debate. That attitude often results in humiliating scenes.

So has artistic commitment become impossible? On the contrary, I am convinced that art must take on a commitment, but not directly a political one. If art is to play a role of importance in the world, it will first have to shake off the nostalgic urge to repeat the mistakes of the past.

The most important political protest movement at the moment is without a doubt the anti-globalization movement. That movement certainly issues a challenge to art too, but it would be wrong to suppose that it is an invitation to activism and pamphleteering. Behind the political commitment of that movement, which is often illogical and lacking a clear target, lies a deeper dissatisfaction, one that cannot be simply translated into slogans and texts on banners. That dissatisfaction is the product of the feeling that the process of globalization, no matter how elusive it may be, robs the world of its profundity, that consumerism as an ideology of salvation not only covers up economic inequality and produces real victims, but also dims our awareness by presenting us with a purely superficial world. The symbol of both that economic totalitarianism and that deliberate numbing of our consciousness is the logo.

It is that logo that presents the biggest challenge to the artist today. It is the artist's task to breathe new life into a world that is felt to be dead and jaded, to explore what opposition an individual can put up to mass culture. Artists are better equipped than anyone else to investigate how the endless flow of artificial sensations produced by the mass culture is related to their own experiences.

That is what I mean by commitment. Let soap actors save the seals. Packing bundles of food for Sarajevo is not a job for artists, but for everybody. Human consciousness and human experience constitute the artist's domain. Now that that domain is in danger of being swept away by a global movement that aims at banal uniformity and generalised experiences as its goal, there is a role for artists to play in the world again. They fulfil that role as they always have: through the strength of their imagination.

Innocuous involvement

The new legitimacy of a design profession

This past August, the world's design elite gathered for the 53rd year in a row in Aspen, a ski resort in the US state of Colorado. Against the backdrop of a Bob Ross painting – a mountain ridge capped with snow dabbed on the canvas in thin dollops of titanium white with a palette knife, and pine trees shooting out the ground using the fan brush – speakers and audiences, in the course of a four-day conference, pored over the theme 'Safe: Design Takes on Risk'. Where normally the privileged members of the highest social circles of the United States populate the hotels, restaurants and ski slopes during their Christmas or Spring breaks, designers were now speaking on the new callings of the design profession. Give the citizen security, for his everyday environment is threatening enough. 'Let's make the world a safer place.' Who better than architects and designers to give shape to this fundamental demand of the American president in the environment of everyday life?

The contrast is mortifying. Designers on a mission are hopping along in the tracks of a regime with a mission, and even the odd individual who considers himself a recalcitrant rubbish collector for that regime gets sucked into the rhetoric of the new security. In a luxury holiday resort they plot the great revolution that is to bring peace and justice to the slum townships around Johannesburg and the killing fields of the former Yugoslavia. An American conference organizer cares deeply about the fate of the world, yet advertises the perks of the location on his website in order to help ticket sales: 'Spend four days among mountains and meadows. A perfect setting for a retreat in the midst of one of the world's most beautiful places – there is nothing quite like Aspen in the summer. Arrive early or stay longer, bring your friends and families.'

Through his television courses in painting, Bob Ross would try, every time, to revitalize the dream of this paradise. A babbling brook, a friendly forest, maybe on occasion a rickety lumberjack hut. And always, the majestically ensnowed mountaintops towered in the background: symbols of rock-like steadfastness. Bourgeois virtue, but expressed in its uttermost naturalistic manifestation. Papa-mountain, mama-forest and the water-children at play. Aspen needed only a digital camera to conjure up precisely the same image. A retreat, literally. Backs turned on the big bad world out there. For designers and their families. For common mortals have no place in Aspen – not during and certainly not before or after the design conference.

In order to engineer security, designers will have to mitigate risk. That much was clear from the title of the conference. The message is clear. There is no place in the new world order for the designer of the 1990s out to satisfy purely hedonistic pleasures. His present fellow professional applies his expertise to averting danger, wherever it may be and in whatever way he can.

Of course this was bound to become a subject of discussion in the Unites States. After all, how can we soothe a population which has suddenly had the calamities of the world delivered to its own doorstep and has no idea how to deal with its new victim role? So close to the second anniversary of the attacks on New York and Washington, there was every reason to do so. And because major shifts in the American mood are always immediately shipped on to the cultures of America's friends and enemies, Aspen instantly provided a global theme as well. The fear of one nation has turned into the obsession of the Western world at least: fear of the alien, the unpredictable, that which cannot be either controlled with regulations, conventions or through appropriate diplomatic, economic or military channels or else marginalized. And therefore – in political terms – demands more regulations, more conventions, more repression and especially more control.

I wasn't there. To me the mountains of Colorado are still nothing more than a photo on a website, just as the sufferings of war, in my actual experience, comes down to a television news report on the child soldiers of Liberia, tucked in between an advert for affordable loans and a chat show about involuntary childlessness. Those who were there, however, are announcing the birth of a new star in the design world. Aspen embraced, en masse, a British architect with the perfect brand name of Cameron Sinclair, who devises projects at his firm, Architecture for Humanity, to combat the AIDS epidemic in Africa, for instance. He does this by issuing an international competition for a mobile field hospital. The costs of the project apparently amounted to no more than one dollar per entry, while the political support for his endeavour is impressive. Both Bush and Clinton are supporters of Cameron Sinclair's noble works and find him a valued conversation partner.

This is probably too cynical, and no doubt I am not doing justice to all sorts of people who try with all their heart and soul to use their work as designers to effect genuine change in the human condition. Yet what is it that is actually so amazing about such a competition, besides the fact that so many designers are prepared to make their expertise available in order to ratchet up the Albert Schweitzer quotient of their profession? Surely not the mobile hospital, which has travelled to the battle-fields as part of every army's equipment since time immemorial? Sure not the issue of AIDS or the disaster area that is Africa? What is amazing is the myopia that accompanies this do-goodism. Design a temporary remedy for a far greater problem, namely that of Western manufacturers and governments having artificially kept the cost of medicines so high that until very recently they were simply not available in large parts of the world. The more mobile the hospitals under these conditions, the better. For you will need them in many places and especially in many places at the same time. And if nothing in the interna-tional balance of power changes, the only thing the next compe-tition will be able to call for is mobile makeshift buildings that can also clone themselves, so that their number keeps pace with the rise in patient or victim tallies in all the hotbeds of the world.

The warm reception accorded Sinclair's ideas proves at least one thing. Designers in 2003 are in diligent search of a societal legitimation for their work, no longer seeking it in the nature – let alone the beauty – of their work itself, but rather in the societal role and thus the prestige of their profession. Design is in need of relevance. Something similar took place when the new-media conference 'Doors of Perception' flew designers in from all over the world in jumbo jets to Amsterdam in 1996 to talk about the positive environmental effects of the increasing use of information technology. 'Doors Info-Eco' was exalted in a matter of a few days of lectures and workshops into a new digital religion. The gathering ended in a High Mass for the computer generation, which would no longer spill a single granule of natural resources to satisfy base urges. In sanctified fellowship a minute's silence was observed in honour of a Nigerian activist who had just paid for his struggle against Shell's oil drillings in his country with his life. The news had been plucked off the Internet a short time before. Amsterdam joined in the mourning and celebrated this moment of universal significance.

Over the past several years, alibis have been sought and found time and time again to elevate design above and beyond its basic utilitarian objectives. It is no longer the purview of historians, sociologists and technology sociologists or other scholars to lay open the essence of a utilitarian object within its historical con-text – it is the creators themselves who make their motivations explicit in their work, define the object as well as its meaning, and project a design philosophy within it. There's a philosophy behind every product, and behind a great many philosophy there turns out to be a product as well.

As self-justification, but above all to imbue the object with meaning, designers conceive narratives that are meant to distinguish their creation from the anonymous mass product. Design training institutions such as the Design Academy in Eindhoven have been imparting this strategy to their students for years. We have seldom been treated to so many projects for the homeless, the visually challenged and other vulnerable social groups as during the final examinations at this school. Whoever has a story – and preferably a powerful story – can take a crack at design. A label blessed with marketing success like Droog Design is making a splash internationally by promoting this narrative Dutch product. That is what is called conceptualism, in an obfuscating sense.

In the period of professionalization the Dutch design sector has been going through since the 1960s, an important premise, which had hitherto provided order and oversight, was abandoned. During the preceding decades things had always been set in terms of 'channelled engagement'. A typographer, a book designer, an industrial designer, a textile designer, an interior architect – essentially every conceivable discipline fell under the same social structuring that the rest of the Dutch population experienced. The country had classes but more significantly was divided into 'pillars', primarily into several religious strongholds, and with the later development of industry gradually into more political and philosophical categories.

Socialism, liberalism, Catholicism: for every 'church' in the pre-war Netherlands there was not only a broadcasting corporation, a party, a school, a newspaper and a sport club, but a design movement as well. To every designer, engagement was something group-identified, collective, and self-evident, geared toward the edification of the various sections of the population. The domestic interior expressed the status and mentality of the group. Its printed matter reflected its lofty ambitions for the future. The polarization among the various pillars also justified a differentiation in style, heavily sign-posted if need be. Ideology – whether promulgated in the dogma of Rome, Moscow or Weimar – dominated the ambitions of a designer.

Only when the Netherlands was for the first time dragged into a world war in 1940 did a paradigm shift take place. Philosophical differences proved to be an insufficiently reliable gauge

in weighing right and wrong, which during the occupation was
sometimes literally a matter of life and death. New alliances
were formed between avowed antipodes. Hands were needed to
run the illegal press and falsify ration cards and identity documents, regardless of whether these hands had once held a Bible
or a maypole. At that time, perhaps more than ever before, typo-
graphers were the instrumental 'telegraph operators' between
message and audience, as the legendary French designer A.M.
Cassandre once identified his trade. They coded a vital message
for a receptive audience. However unpleasant it may sound, in
times of need no one has to wonder where the design profession
is supposed to draw its legitimacy, not even when it placed
itself in the service of the occupier.

This distinction between right and wrong continued to be
applied in the years of reconstruction after 1945. The chan-
nelling of engagement may have proceeded along different lines,
but in the world of the so-called 'committed arts' there still
reigned an absolute sense of significance that in actuality had
been defined by choices made during the war years. Designers
such as Piet Zwart had contributed to the blueprint for the
Netherlands rising from the ashes back when the country was
still under occupation, and during the period that followed they
called the shots. In 1929 Zwart had observed that design was
not a question of taste 'but an expression of our attitude toward
life'. This thinking predominated in the post-war period as well.
It proved its relevance not only short after the liberation, but
also seems reflected in the concept of 'mentality' that caught on
midway through the 1990s as a label for the most individualistic
of engagements.

Every professional conception, every product was vetted,
so soon after peace had broken out, as though the Nuremberg
tribunal was again in session. The 'moderates' were if necessary
shipped off to advertising; the 'orthodox' kept watch over the
actual heritage of the soul of modernist Dutch design. It was
the era of Good Housing, of institutions such as the Stedelijk
Museum, under the leadership of former resistance fighter
Willem Sandberg, taking on the challenge of indoctrinating the
public and elevating its tastes. The hunger for culture, which
had stood on the back burner for so long, had to be stilled.

Like the society in which it was rooted, the design community sought a new division of roles. There might have been a
scarcity of everything – paper, building materials, machines,
money and raw materials – but the objective was clear and
unusually communal. On the way toward a healthy democracy
the designer was to be part public servant and part visionary.

Pragmatism and ideology went hand in hand during the Reconstruction. Only now was the way open for the Netherlands to rebuild a genuinely industrial society, in which the exchange of information would be free, the availability of goods universal and every form of tyranny banished for good. In the distance the welfare state glimmered, and designers would help build it. As far as models to be applied were concerned, these were borrowed not only from the fundamental European principles of Bauhaus and the 'New Objectivity' of Dutch functionalism, but also from insights and theories that had been shaped in America.

This is precisely what the young professionals of the 1960s and '70s did. The period of scarcity seemed over for good. In graphic design circles especially, the expansion of economic welfare saw a trickling away of the unidirectional aspect of the trade. The strict differentiation between the commercial confrères and their ideological counterparts was still paid lip service, but in practice it was much harder to detect. Traditional engagement, the quintessential domain of this latter group, at times was out of balance with the drive toward scale expansion and professionalization of the first true design firms to develop in the Netherlands. They were no longer content with the patronage of the government, of the odd enlightened manufacturer or cultural institution. Only market expansion could allow them to strengthen and subsequently consolidate their position.

A trend-setting firm like Total Design was able to make the leap and pulled other design firms in its wake. On the remnants of social engagement they constructed a philosophy that was much more motivated from the practice of the trade itself. Systems theory made its debut in graphic design practice. Method became more important than expression, as had in actuality been taught at the Ulm School of Design since the late 1950s. In 1984, co-founder Tómas Maldonado recalled the ambitions of this school: 'The driving force behind our curiosity, our researches and our theoretical efforts was the desire to provide a solid theoretical basis for design. Admittedly, this was an exceedingly ambitious resolution. We were attempting to force a change in the design world that was comparable to the process by which alchemy mutated into chemistry. This attempt, we now know, was premature.'[1]

Total Design succeeded where Ulm had failed, perhaps for the very reason that the firm operated essentially operated without ideology, while the school got bogged down in the compulsion toward a political stand. This conflict also marked the new watershed in the Dutch design community. Designers with

a social mission drifted back to commissions from mostly the
cultural and activist world; the commercially minded allied
themselves with the rapidly growing communications industry
and endeavoured to carve out as high a position as possible
within it. In terms of the early twenty-first century, for the first
time (at least a portion of) the design community bowed to the
primacy of the economy. Those who refused to go along were in
fact condemned to adopt an adversary position. As a personal
act. The legitimacy of the profession was derived from the
market, or else from the anti-market. It turned into a choice
between relative invisibility – firms like Total Design have contributed in a significant way to growing anonymity in Dutch
design – and the enlargement of the individual signature.

Engagement as lifetime employment proved initially more
sustainable, as it happened, in the anonymous circuit than in
the adversary position. The communications industry managed
to appropriate the radical jargon of the individualists in increasingly clever ways. What today might still be a personal statement
might tomorrow be absorbed into the mainstream of commercial
communication. And so the individualist would repeatedly confront the same choice: either develop new avenues by cultivating
new commitments or else succumb to the temptations of the
jackpot. Diving into the economic maelstrom might well lead to
a marginalized role for the designer – one reason why co-founder
Benno Wissing eventually left Total Design, for instance. Or else
once again go in search of the fringe of society and from there
launch the next surprise attack. It was in such a climate that
the international manifesto 'First Things First' had been issued
as early as 1964. A call for a design trade that would set its
talents, power and influence to use for worthier causes than
flogging cat food.

However, 'First Things First' made very little essential change to
the status quo. So little that 35 years later it proved necessary
to publish a second, updated version of the manifesto. The new
media had made their debut, and with that a new platform had
been created for a newer form of activism. Commercial and
technological structures had become so dominant that it was
now pointless to turn one's back on them. Those who wanted to
challenge the system could only do so from within the system
itself. Those who wanted to fully exploit the system ostensibly
positioned themselves outside of it.

That is the reality of the 1990s. Bennetton as activist; the
independent publisher as a market factor. Those who operated
within the system – whether or not with the ambition to sub-

vert it – could make use of the multitude of niches in the abundant supply of information. With – but in most cases without – ideology. Resistance had once again become a cultural act, a figure of speech that at most found legitimacy in great concepts such as anti-globalization or sustainability. Far more often, the counter-movement, certainly in the Netherlands, was fed by an enlargement of the design personality. The critical position became one of personal commitment to the development of one's own area of expertise, of the technique or the status of communication. Interesting for who might wish to see it, but certainly not related to a clear societal position.[2]

Many forms of public engagement had since become utterly innocuous. They preach to the choir, or are deployed as a toothless feel-good factor. The more the designer began to define his role as an editor – subordinated the claim on the form to his claim on the content – the more naïve, sadly, communication became. Never before had the designer as a person, as well as his own motivations, been so thoroughly the alpha and omega of his work. Great themes occasionally served as useful alibis in this regard – as they are for Cameron Sinclair, or for the artist Lucy Orta, who in response to the growing refugee problem designed an individual garment of waterproof plastic. Her shiny silver tent is fitted with a hood that just barely allows the refugee to breathe. This is how we rid the world of suffering and in the meantime stay true to our personal sense of aesthetics. What gorgeous refugees we'll get out of it.

Notes

1   'The legacy of the School of Ulm', in *Rassegna* VI 19/3, Sett. 1984.

2   See Jouke Kleerebezem, 'De vervreemding aan de macht' ('Alienation takes over'), *Items*, nr. 4, 2000, p. 41. He writes: 'A new generation of designers is for the moment untroubled by existential angst [unlike their radical predecessors from the 1960s, GS]. Everyday life, after all, changes even without the restricted awareness of revolutionary resistance – sometimes, even, fastest under the influence of commercial ambitions or technological innovations.'

Digital engagement

José van Dijck

> Radio is the medium for frenzy, and has been the major means
> of hotting up the tribal blood of Africa, India and China, alike.
> TV has cooled down Cuba, as it is cooling down America.
> What the Cubans are getting by TV is the experience of being
> directly engaged in the making of political decisions.
> Marshall McLuhan, *Understanding Media*

McLuhan wrote these words in 1964, when his book *Under-standing Media* bewitched the world with mantras such as 'the global village' and 'the medium is the message'. The theories formulated by this Canadian media guru maintain that the nature of a medium determines the political involvement of citizens and that there is a causal relationship between the kind of technology and the form of public participation in the nation state. McLuhan used the terms 'hot' and 'cool' (albeit quite inconsistently) to denote the causal relationship between medium and engagement. A medium like radio is 'hot', which means that it *causes frenzy*, that it invites *pluralistic* opinions, and necessarily encourages *participation*. The medium of television, on the other hand, is 'cool', induces *passivity*, but leads to great *solidarity* (uniqueness) and results in *involvedness*. In McLuhan's eyes, engagement is something heterogeneous: the subtle gradations of the rich palette are pluralism *and* solidarity, participation *and* involvement, heated opposition *and* passive acquiescence. He concludes, '… it is such uniqueness and diversity that can be fostered under electric conditions as never before.'

To our modern ears, these pronouncements of the 1960s now sound as hilarious as they do surprising, but, in the 1980s and '90s, McLuhan's technological, deterministic vision found plenty of resonance among new digital prophets. McLuhan would have undoubtedly ranked the computer and the Internet in the same class as the radio: a hot medium that gives a voice to many different 'tribes' and leads to active participation. More specifically, in the early years of the Internet boom, it was not unusual to hear the Internet being compared to the radio in order to sound the praises of this new medium above the passivity of that other mass medium: the television. As in the early years of radio, Internet led to the formation of new communities of people who shared specific interests and thus bridged geographical distance. Michael Heim and Howard Rheingold wrote enthusiastically about how digital media stimulated the social involvement of citizens and how all kinds of 'online communities' developed via the Internet. With just as much passion as McLuhan, they argued that the digital culture would lead to more social enthusiasm about, and greater involvement in, democratic processes.

There are still politicians and scholars who perceive an undeniable link between the preferred medium of certain groupings and the form of their political involvement. Television, for example, is supposed to foster a sense of unity in Europe due to its straightforward reporting from the political hubs of power, for example meetings between EU leaders or a G8 summit. The anti-globalists, on the other hand, mobilize and inform their supporters primarily via the Internet, and thanks to this medium they are able to sound the 'tam-tam' (McLuhan's term) – the various voices of the opposition – noisily. Engagement is therefore translated in the preferred media of the establishment versus those of the anti-establishment.

No matter how attractive such a simple explanation might be, it is based on a great many incorrect assumptions, three of which I will explore further. Firstly, technology, and thus digital technology, is not the cause of engagement. I would be equally justified in arguing that the actions of anti-globalists are made possible by cheap airline tickets rather than the Internet, or that the introduction of the Euro, more than television reporting, has advanced the European sense of unification. The massive explosion in digital media is not nourished by a growing desire for engagement, nor has the dawn of Internet, e-mail, mobile telephones and SMS positively influenced our involvement with or enthusiasm for society. The fact that schoolchildren spend hours every day surfing the Internet is no indicator of an increased interest in the public sphere, though it speaks volumes about their desire to communicate and keep abreast of trends. Unfortunately, we all too easily confuse the need for interpersonal contact with engagement, though they are not the same thing by any means.

Secondly, a new virtual space does not automatically create a new public sphere. McLuhan was correct in regarding pluriformity and solidarity as two necessary aspects of the public sphere. Initially, the Internet seemed to make an idyllic new world possible, one in which every group would have its own place beneath the digital sun. It soon turned out that the hierarchy and patterns of the real public space applied in cyberspace as well. Over the years, another grudge has arisen:

the Internet, precisely because it promoted the fragmentation of the public debate, would never be able to lead to unanimity and thus effective action. The Internet creates distance rather than fostering involvement and solidarity. After all, adding your name to an electronic protest e-mail is just as 'engaged' as putting your signature on a pre-printed payment slip for Greenpeace. There are, of course, countless examples of groups for which the Internet has been crucial to their formation and continuation. In practically every case, however, the medium's function was instrumental. The Internet will never be a substitute for public space, at best an extra overflow that is complementary to the 'real' public space.

Thirdly, the degree of interactivity that a particular medium stimulates is no indication of the participation of its users in political culture or public debate. It is commercial organizations which are best able to exploit interactive media, and prompt large masses of people to participate actively. The example of *Idols* is still fresh in our memories: a successful campaign by a commercial broadcaster to involve large numbers of teenagers by means of SMS messaging, e-mail reactions and digi-events. It was intended neither to collect their opinions nor to have them take part in a discussion, but to generate cash; it was not meant to stimulate involvement, but to mobilize fans and consumers. Interactivity has, in this instance, nothing to do with engagement in the sense of social involvement. Here it is about nothing else but participation in a capitalist economy, where the exchange of opinions and communication is increasingly mediated by capital-intensive and thus profit-generating technology.

'Digital engagement' is a non sequitur: the first word has no logical or causal link to the second. Does this then mean that there is no digital engagement in which digital technology and involvement with the public sphere are closely intertwined? In fact there is. Over recent years, a growing group of scholars and technologists has been emphatically highlighting the way in which digital technology dominates the public domain and steers society and social life in specific directions, often without us being aware of it. Politics, or ideology, is ensconced *within* technology, as it were. How is the exchange of ideas among people involved in public debate increasingly controlled by Microsoft's software or Intel's chips? How do Google and other search engines regulate our demand for information? Will we hand over full control of the distribution of our cultural heritage and access to our intellectual capital to Silicon Valley? This sort of digital engagement does not take its cue from the inherent pros and cons of technology, but from the invisible power that digital technologies and enterprises have gained in the private domain and in collective culture.

The champions and advocates on principle of so-called *peer-to-peer* technologies (P2P) seem to be profoundly concerned with the pillars of our democracy; they are dedicated to the design and refinement of software and hardware that enables people to communicate and express themselves creatively without the necessary means belonging to a small commercial elite. Designers of P2P systems such as Gnutella, Freenet, Jabber, Napster, and many others, have steadfastly held high the principle that software must be free of patents and that it must be refined through its use by communities. Peer-to-peer software itself is in the public domain, thus preventing companies from gaining exclusive power over content or distribution.

The creation and distribution of cultural products, such as music, books and films, is also increasingly dominated by technology and commerce. Professors of law such as Lawrence Lessig (Stanford Law School) are at the forefront of a movement that calls into question our growing dependence on commercial software. The future of our cultural and intellectual capital, Lessig argues in *The Future of Ideas* (2001), is increasingly controlled by multinational corporations like Microsoft and America Online, which now own the lion's share of all the copyrights on images and which they cash in on. The use and creative re-use of cultural products has, of old, been a source of inspiration, yet it is now becoming increasingly restricted thanks to strictly enforced patent and copyright laws, at the expense of the public domain where the exchange of creative and political expression should be free.

In these cases, engagement means that those concerned are taking aim at the technology itself. Rather than being a *medium* of political engagement or social involvement, digital technology forms the *casus belli* for the struggle to keep the public domain public. Instead of talking about hot or cool media, as McLuhan did, people like Lessig should show how the misuse of digital media can make someone white-hot, while their use should certainly not leave anyone icy-cold.

Public role of architecture under pressure

Janny Rodermond

The world of architecture is constantly looking for new ideas and innovative design visions. For a long time the role of an avant-garde was linked to the modernist belief in progress. Commitment implied working towards emancipation, the creation of equal domestic, working and living conditions, and the construction of cities in which there was a place for everyone. Modernism is now viewed by architects and critics as 'heritage', as something of the past, as can be seen from the contributions to the 2002 publication *Back from Utopia. The Challenge of the Modern Movement.*[1] The views of designers, academics and critics from many different countries assembled there show the diversity of the heritage of modernism. It is almost a magic mirror in which everyone can project the Utopia of his or her choice. Hilde Heynen argues there for a continuation of the critical attitude inherent in modernism instead of thoughtlessly casting it aside. The object of that critique falls outside the scope of the book, but it is important for the continued existence of the design disciplines that the question should be raised in teaching and practice of *which* society is being built. The uncritical acceptance of commissions undermines the discipline's own field of work as well as the public role of architecture. The question is now whether designers can also reflect on the future at a time of economic stagnation and a strict containment of the belief in progress. What alternatives are there to nostalgia for an idealised past or to an overdose of pragmatism?

At the moment the end of the international hype about the exceptional quality of Dutch architecture is having a paralyzing effect on the design world. While the media are full of discussions by critics, academics and journalists about the demise of the welfare state, the consequences of an expanding Europe, and the less positive consequences of globalization and privatization, the architects are seldom heard. Even when it is a question of topics more directly related to their own field of operations, such as the new housing shortage or the problem of safety in public spaces that features so prominently on the political agenda, architects do not seem to have any public statements to make. Typical characteristics of a hype are its temporary nature and a certain lack of content, so its end did not come as a surprise. Nevertheless, it is remarkable how the vitality of architecture could drain away in such a short time. Perhaps the cause of the current dullness is the fact that the success of Dutch architecture was based on its capacity to enthusiastically flesh out the latest modernization.[2] Deregulation and privatization went hand in hand with the plan of an architectural policy aimed at encouraging the aestheticization of the cities and the countryside. Architects from the Netherlands could be deployed anywhere in the world because of their ability to translate the far-reaching economization of society into design studies, experimental buildings and spectacular future scenarios that appealed to the imagination, based on the extrapolation of a dizzying mass of data. Now that the economy is in recession, the building market is stagnant, and the parties who place the commissions are no longer interested in seductive settings for greedy customers, it is not realistic to sit back and wait for the golden days to come back. It is urgently necessary to think about the function of architecture in the new economic and social context.

Architects are faced with a dilemma. In order to claim the special position of the profession as the defender of public interests, they will have to engage in the debate on the demise of the collective sector. To be able to exercise the profession of architect in the Netherlands, you have to be enrolled in the Register of Architects.[3] Architecture shapes the public space and partly determines how it functions. Access to care, education and housing for everyone is a matter of concern for the design sector too. Now that the public sector is under pressure, a critical debate on the limits of privatization is called for. If architects opt to act as ambassadors of collective interests, they may have to discard the allies who laid the financial basis for their success in the 1990s. In the early 1990s Sharon Zukin already pointed out that architecture in the United States had been colonized by the private sector and that architects could therefore not be expected to resist the domination of economic objectives.[4] In the Netherlands, where the private sector is also involved in the proper functioning of the cities, public and private interests are more intertwined. Nevertheless, there is a danger of an essential erosion of the sphere of operations of the Dutch architects if they fail to unravel the complexity of spatial issues. Now that the panels in politics and economics have shifted, the sector is obliged to determine its own agenda and on that basis to exercise an influence on its political and social context. Commitment to the social issues is thus more than a new trend; it is the *raison d'être* of the public function of architecture.

The fragile society

Recently we are increasingly being told that society is not man-made. That is a ready excuse to evade serious problems. Architecture directly intervenes in people's lives. That is why the widespread discontent that was manifested during the Dutch elections of 2002 is something that should be a matter of concern to architects. Architecture has only too readily floated on the waves of a prosperous economy without wanting to consider the other side of the coin. Its international success was based precisely on a carefree optimism. The architecture of the 'second modernism' acted as a lubricant for far-reaching transformations and obscured the relations of power that accompanied globalization and privatization. Architecture went along with and profited from the de-ideologisation of thought.[5] After the fall of the Berlin Wall, after all, there still seemed to be a workable model for society left, namely democratic capitalism. The worldwide competition between cities functioned as a catalyst for the many transformations and expansions, thereby creating plenty of work for a growing number of architectural practices. Collaborating on this modernisation was progressive. After all, in the end the economic growth would increase the prosperity of everybody in the world.

This optimism was unfounded. Democracy both presupposes and cherishes equality.[6] Capitalism, on the other hand, not only presupposes inequality, it creates it. The consequences of this are now visible in the rich countries and cities too. What used to be marginal groups are manifesting themselves more and more in the centre of the culture and economy of the West and are demanding a place in it. This implies large-scale migration. In the cities this is accompanied by, among other things, segregation, a phenomenon that has hit the headlines in the Netherlands.[7] The sociologist Gabriel van den Brink describes Dutch society as a class society in which 30 per cent still has a low level of education, earns a low wage, cannot keep up with modern life, and is morally at sea.[8] This group – which does not consist exclusively of non-Dutch citizens – is confronted the most violently with the problems of a multicultural society, crime, and the collapse of public services. These are the citizens under threat, who voiced their dissatisfaction on a large scale by voting for the LPF party in 2002. According to Van den Brink, half of the population consists of the contented middle class, while he sees the rest as the cosmopolitan citizens of the world who are able to stand up for themselves and for whom all the changes cannot proceed fast enough. These successful citizens have no idea of how the rest of society lives. There is thus not much understanding of the way in which the dissatisfaction is manifested. Van den Brink: 'The problem of the future is not the political commitment of the citizen. The problem is the gap between the committed citizen and the actions of the professional managers in The Hague. If that gap is not bridged, the commitment will not take on form.'

Van den Brink sees a task for the 'public professionals' – people who are professionally involved with social problems through their work and are concerned about the public interest – in removing the obstacles between the committed citizens and the administrators. He argues for a revival of the culture of the citizen, without falling back on old traditions and models, since they must be constantly reinvented. Architects can assume the responsibility of making clear to what extent the discontent of the citizens is connected with the environment they live in. If the existing citizen commitment to city or society is not given a form, a large percentage of the population will give up. This is a threat to the functioning of democracy, Van den Brink argues. His analysis is a plea to widen political decision-making.

The commitment that is required of professionals today is not some watered-down version of the 1960s. The liberal democracy that is now regularly raised for discussion may not be ideal, but for the time being there is no better alternative for a system based on the acceptance of cultural diversity on the basis of equality before the law. Society cannot be moulded according to a certain model, and we should not want to mould it in that way either, since that presupposes that it can be completely controlled from a particular point. Still, society does require attention and maintenance, in interaction with all the groups that form a part of it. Architects often move in international circles. This should not stop them from sitting down with residents at the same time to discuss the renewal of the neighbourhood they live in. Familiarity with global developments is necessary in order to place the local-level processes within the present-day political and economic frameworks. Commitment entails a lot of knowledge and an open attitude towards different views and life-styles. An international orientation is essential in an expanding, multicultural Europe.

A multicultural society is not concerned with reinforcing or purging identities. That is not the way to bring about dialogue. Sjoerd de Jong calls for the umbrella concept of culture to be broken down into political, social, economic, religious and moral factors.[9] It is not a question of discovering cultural essences or introducing abstract hierarchies, but of an ongoing,

rational inquiry into human similarities and differences.
Charting the different layers of the world around us is an
important precondition for successful interventions in complex
urban housing zones.

The Utopia of safety

Thinking in economic terms dominates Dutch local and national
politics. However, town and country planning cannot be completely subsumed within such a framework, simply because this
plays down values other than economic ones. That is why architects and urban planners are faced every day with the challenge
of defending values that cannot be expressed in monetary
terms: not just the importance of the public space, the appearance of buildings in the urban landscape, the innovation of
urban functions, beauty and sustainability, but also differentiation in housing, the construction of school premises, municipal
offices, police stations, law courts, hospitals and health centres
that can fulfil their function as important public services in
society. It was precisely because of the success of Dutch architecture that hardly any attempts were made in the 1990s to
register the changes actually taking place in the cities. Local
authorities focused on large-scale projects and building homes
for the upper segment of the market. At the local level too, the
idea was that favourable economic statistics would automatically lead to an improvement in the living conditions of every
sector of the population. The prediction of an 'upward flow' in
housing is a good example.

One of the butts of citizen dissatisfaction at the moment is
the mentality in public administration that only leaves room
for what can be expressed in monetary terms, according to F.R.
Ankersmit.[10] Within that perspective, it is difficult to determine
political priorities, since that presupposes thinking in terms of
objectives, which in turn requires a cultural framework. One
option is to resign oneself to accepting that the demise of the
modern state is an inevitable stage in history, Ankersmit states,
but it can also be maintained that history is not fate. After all,
that would mean the end of all politics worthy of the name, of
freedom, democracy, political propriety, political accountability,
and our ability to shape our collective future ourselves. A
warning of this kind ought to make the design sector think,
because if this scenario becomes fact, what will be left of that
sector's field of operations?

In connection with citizen unrest, a debate was opened in
the Netherlands about norms and values. This was not based
on an analysis of the causes of that dissatisfaction, but was

aimed at containing its negative consequences. The debate resulted in many cases in attempts to tie citizens to specific rules of behaviour. Norms and values form part of cultures. The so-called debate was primarily deployed by those who initiated it to impose a particular view of culture on citizens with different cultural backgrounds. This striving for dominance is motivated by fear. The processes of segregation at work in the cities are considered to be a natural phenomenon that threatens the citizens' welfare and should therefore be rendered harmless. Such reflexes stand in the way of an inquisitive attitude towards the potential of metropolitan diversity. Strategies that deny the migration of people in search of safety and prosperity ignore phenomena that are the inevitable partners of globalisation. Migration presupposes an open-mindedness, based on the mutual exchange of information and respect.

The measure of how much the appreciation of freedom and the obsession with safety are connected with one another has been described in detail by Hans Boutellier.[11] He explains why safety occupies such a central position in political thought. The constant search for safety, he argues, is a utopia. It is unattainable, no matter how much effort the government makes. It expresses a dissatisfaction, but above all a desire as well. Boutellier warns of the totalitarian nature of utopian thought. He distinguishes two strategies in the attainment of safety. The first is based on repression, and is attractive to politicians because it is in line with populist solutions to social tensions. The second is more complex and is strongly linked to local processes. In the last resort it is a question of achieving social cohesion in combination with the freedom to opt for individual convictions and life-styles. To avoid the emergence of a 'culture of control', Boutellier argues for moral reflection, a renewed formation of local communities, a strengthening of the ability to empathise, and a reappraisal of the cold and calculating market mentality.

The obsession with security penetrates every sphere of life and calls for a constant drawing of physical or regulated borders. They are reflected in all kinds of functions, from the width of the stairs on a staircase and the distance between one home and another to the fully controlled construction of large-scale infrastructural works. Security necessitates the division of activities and life-styles, protection and isolation. Security is the basis for segregation in the urban regions and erodes the basis of a minimal form of social cohesion. Designers can track down the negative consequences of the Utopia of safety and help to look for alternatives. Thinking about and shaping a better world has been an important component of architecture since modernism. If the second wave of modernism has been able to put architecture in the number one position internationally because it was so good at matching the forces of globalization and privatisation, the time has now come for the next stage. The freedom implicit in the second wave of modernism runs up against its limitations in the striving for security. Boutellier argues that they presuppose one another. A broad cultural perspective is called for to give this form at the local level, and designers cannot fall back on models or market-orientated life-styles at this point. The challenge is to contribute to the building of cities in which the residents can feel both at home and cosmopolitan.

More than visual culture

In their search for a new interpretative framework, various architects and critics have explored the field of visual culture during the last few years.[12] The contribution that this makes to thinking about architecture is disappointing, if not misleading. The perspective of visual culture is simply too limited. Of course, architecture can be a part of visual culture, for instance when the façades are used to conceal the poverty of a standard building; then architecture has sunk to the level of façade design to cover what Rem Koolhaas has called 'junk space' – impoverished buildings with a limited shelf life. Architects can deliberately deploy the image to communicate something: the identity or the logo of an enterprise or city. When it comes to this form of branding, 'contemporary' architecture is just as effective as historicising design. Besides, architecture often appears in the media too as the production of images. In that case the perspective on architecture is primarily aesthetic, but this offers too few possibilities for analysing the challenges facing architecture today.

Culture is more than visual culture. It is also more than the ensemble of cultural sectors, more than the sum total of the life-styles of cultural groups, and more than the collection of cultural heritage. Culture is first and foremost living culture: what characterises our society, what supports our ideals and cherishes our wishes and desires. It is at the same time the framework within which we can place all these factors, a framework that calls for renewal of the foundations and an appreciable widening of the field of vision. To get to grips with the global phenomena of today, it is necessary to rewrite history from the present-day perspective of globalization, migration, and growing inequality.[13] Trade, education, tourism and other activities offer a basis for the exchange of knowledge with other cultures. New frames of thought are needed from which we can determine our position in place and time. This calls for a curious profession. Only by building up a multi-faceted knowledge will we be able to comprehend the positive and negative consequences of globalization in relation to one another.

The German sociologist Gerhard Schulze, who analysed the experience society in 1992, recently published a book with the ambitious title *Die Beste Aller Welten, Wohin bewegt sich die Gesellschaft im 21. Jahrhundert?* which contains a well-founded plea for the strengthening of a broad cultural education.[14] Schulze tries to form a picture of the future; thinking about the future is part of the field of operations of the modernists, among whose ranks Schulze also belongs. But while in the previous century this thought was strongly tied to the expansion of the technological possibilities and the related economic growth, culture will be the decisive factor in the twenty-first century, he argues. This is not to say that the science of nature and technology has had its day, but its further development will inevitably involve the making of culturally determined choices. The more we are able to do, the question of what we actually want becomes increasingly prominent. It is impossible to summarize Schulze's large-scale study. The most striking feature is his claim that there is a lack of everyday cultural knowledge. For instance, debates are often characterised by partiality, fascination with extremes, and a fixation on events instead of processes. Those taking part in debates base their arguments more on their own perceptions than on listening and exchanging ideas. Schulze notes a far-reaching anarchy in the construction of arguments, the lack of explicit criteria of evaluation, the inability to distinguish between good and bad arguments, between correct and false empirical perceptions, and between explanatory and obfuscatory concepts.

The answer to the question of how we want to live presupposes a way of thinking in which people, not matter, occupy pride of place. This is not to say that culture is a private affair. As a sociologist, Schulze places emphasis precisely on what is common to us all and on what is ordinary. Everyday life is constructed, not found, he claims, even though this usually takes place unconsciously. History is thus not fate in his view, and society can still be moulded. However, he argues, at the moment culture lacks coherent systems of concepts and the capacity to use them, the ability to abstract, the mastery of the basic principles of a logical argument, and the ability to reflect. It is not the multicultural society that Schulze sees as a problem, but the lack of basic cultural knowledge. He thus distances himself from the issues of the day and places his stakes on a change of perspective. Beside the perspective that is based on technological progress and economic growth, he sets a second perspective that is necessary in order to reflect on the direction in which societies are heading. He marks out the twenty-first century for the elaboration of this cultural perspective. We can get started right away.

Notes

1 Hubert-Jan Henket and Hilde Heynen (eds.) *Back from Utopia, The Challenge of the Modern Movement*. 010 Publishers, Rotterdam 2002.

2 Janny Rodermond, 'De stoffering van het poldermodel. Architectuur en stedenbouw in tijden van deregulering', in: *de Architect*, 1997, no.10, pp. 38-44. Also published in English as 'Furnishing the Polder Model. Architecture and Urbanism in an Age of Deregulation', in: Hans Ibelings (ed.) *The Artificial Landscape. Contemporary architecture, urbanism, and landscape architecture in the Netherlands*, NAi Publishers, Rotterdam 2000, pp. 263-265.

3 This legitimizes, among other things, the necessary condition for practising architects to be enrolled in the Register of Architects, so that there is a quality check on access by new members of the profession.

4 Sharon Zukin, *Landscapes of Power, From Detroit to Disney World*, University of California Press, Los Angeles 1991.

5 K. Michael Hays, 'Het ontstaan van ideologische gladheid. Waar het opheffen van de architectonische autonomie toe kan leiden', in: *de Architect,* 1995, no. 12, pp. 24-27.

6 Michael Kinsley, 'Kapitalisme en democratie: de tandem hapert', *NRC Handelsblad*, 12 June 2003.

7 Frederiek Weeda, 'Scheiding naar ras en klasse is volledig. Onderzoek naar onderwijs Amsterdam', *NRC Handelsblad*, 26 August 2003.

8 Gabriel van den Brink, *Mondiger of moeilijker? Een studie naar de habitus van hedendaagse burgers*. SDU uitgevers, The Hague 2002. Tom-Jan Meeus, 'De opstand is niet voorbij. Politiek en openbaar bestuur moeten radicaal hervormen', interview with Gabriel van den Brink in *NRC Handelsblad* 28/29 December 2002.

9 Sjoerd de Jong, 'Gelijker dan de rest. Cultuurrelativisme en de ware westerse normen', *NRC Handelsblad* 10 October 2002.

10 F.R. Ankersmit. 'Nieuw elan voor een vormloze zak meel', *NRC Handelsblad*, 5 January 2003.

11 Hans Boutellier, *De veiligheidsutopie. Hedendaags onbehagen en*

verlangen rond misdaad en straf. Boom Juridische uitgevers, The Hague 2002.

12   The architectural journal *Archis* includes the words 'Visual Culture' in its subtitle. The theme of the Architecture in the Netherlands Yearbook 2002-03 was 'visual culture'. This theme is introduced by Roemer van Toorn with the essay 'Propaganda and the return of ornament'. NAi Publishers, Rotterdam 2003.

13   Okwui Enwezor, 'The Black Box', in: *Documenta 11_Platform 5*, exh.cat., Hatje Cantz, Ostfildern-Ruit 2002 pp. 42-55.

14   Gerhard Schulze, *Die beste Aller Welten, Wohin bewegt sich die Gesellchaft im 21.Jahrhundert?* Carl Hanser Verlag, Munich/Vienna 2003.

New commitment at the crossroads

Ton Verstegen

In the July 2003 issue of *Schooldomein* [School Domain],
Syb van Breda, an architect with Royal Haskoning Architecten,
pinpoints three trends within the ongoing increase of scale in
secondary and higher professional education.[1] The first is the
rise of the calculating student who zaps and shops at various
institutions. This forces schools to compete and to pay a lot of
attention to their image and accessibility. Second, he notes an
increasing pressure to be efficient: the courses have to keep
offering more and more variants and facilities on tighter
budgets. Third, he states that many teachers consider large-
scale premises to be detrimental to education – a problem that
is particularly acute when it comes to the integration of several
formerly autonomous schools in a new organisation. That
accounts for the call for small and sustainable. Van Breda
concludes: 'The demand for the spatial expression of smallness
of scale, individual recognisability and intimacy will increase,
though hand in hand with increasingly strict demands with
respect to efficiency and functionality'.

At first sight the trends towards an increase of scale and
a decrease of scale seem to be incompatible. This is where Van
Breda conjures up a genuine *deus ex machina*: new premises.
New premises mean the confirmation of the brave new world
'in which everything is no longer what it was'. And new premises
provide the opportunity for a new breeding-ground for the new
culture that has to be created after the mergers.

Starting in the 1980s, schools in the Netherlands have increasingly followed the model of the world of industry and commerce.
Lessons were renamed contact hours, classes became budget-
ary items, permanent appointments became flexible units of
full-time employment, new studies became efficient learning
trajectories, accounts were settled on the basis of productivity
statistics, and the classical school building went out of fashion
because it contained too much unutilised space. The knowledge
culture became the knowledge economy.[2] The image of the
zapping and shopping student, based on that of the consumer,
fitted in with this too. Thus the picture gradually emerged of the
school as a department store where students pick and choose
their knowledge, assisted by advisers who train the customers
in how to be successful in this universe of possibilities. Central

direction by the government has been abolished. Schools have become well-managed enterprises with their own hierarchy of administrators and managers.

The increase of scale is part of the large modernization project that did not really get under way in the Netherlands until after the Second World War. This led in the 1960s to the first wave of increase of scale, with gigantic educational premises for which the architects thought up robust Modernist forms. Small-scale design was introduced in the early 1970s, for which the architects had a Structuralist solution. Since then aspirations have merely increased, and architecture is no exception. School premises must strengthen identities and beat the competition. They must give young people the feeling that they are participants in progress: the brave new world of high tech and the crystal palace. And they must also help to create a new culture: a sense of community and security within a small group.

From the first, architects in the Netherlands have adjusted to the demands as closely as possible. The increase in scale was accepted as something inevitable. Still, architecture could also prevent the individual from being swallowed up by the crowd. Van Breda's article is an invitation to tackle the new challenge in the same spirit. That challenge is: 'Big is Beautiful / Small is Beautiful'. Architects, rise dauntlessly to the bifurcation and take it up! It also seems to be an invitation to the new generation of architects in the Netherlands who have managed to discover an advantage in every disadvantage and an opportunity in every problem. The success of this approach has now apparently filtered through to the architects who are associated with the big consultancy firms and to the columns of *School-domein*, a 'magazine for the perfect learning, working and living environment'.[3]

That the increase of scale works can no doubt be demonstrated with higher productivity figures and a strong increase in the number of studies. So why is it that education primarily evokes a picture of permanent crisis: fraud with numbers of students and productivity, dumbing down, the shortage of teachers, the avoidance of difficult studies?

Increase of scale is not purely a success story. Awareness of this has led, particularly in Germany, to the demand for a second modernism, a reflexive modernism.[4] Modernisation automatically produces an awareness of its own limitations, the idea runs, and thus of its own limits. It divides itself in two and brings forth a second modernity. Modernism becomes reflexive, its completeness consists of accepting its incompleteness. In the Netherlands the only area where traces of this progressive insight can be found is in agriculture.[5] It has apparently not yet reached the field of education. And what about architecture?

It is noteworthy that the architecture of the Netherlands was put forward in Germany a few years ago as an example of an architecture appropriate to a modernism that has become reflexive.[6] To judge from the article by Ullrich Schwarz, that is no longer the case. The generic, supermodern or datascape architecture is characterised, in his view, by a 'shrill subordination' to the economic demands of globalization and a 'compromising stylistic uniformity'.[7] A reflexive architecture, according to Schwarz, goes beyond form, it is an architecture that accommodates the unspecific and the incomplete. It is not out to improve life by imposing form from the outside. It wants to become everyday and thereby to address the stock of possibilities that are latent in that everydayness. Schwarz refers to a turning of prose into poetry in this connection.

Both the German praise and the criticism of the architecture of the Netherlands seem exaggerated to me. The datascapes, generic containers and even the neutral supermodernist boxes embody more irony, surrealism, poetry and relativisation of self than one might expect. The scapes are not just the virtuoso act that resolves all contradictory demands with a sweeping gesture. That act is partly played with an awareness that it can never be completely true, and should thus not be taken too literally. The scapes are virtual forms that have been excavated from everyday reality and are intended to turn that reality into poetry. The same goes for the word containers like 'Bigness' that Rem Koolhaas uses. These metaphors romantically bring about a 'systematic idealisation, a spontaneous overestimation of what there is'.[8]

This architecture lies somewhere between subordination and irony, between a laconic acceptance of the everyday and its poetic recharging. In her lecture 'Ästhetische Globalisierung' [Aesthetic Globalisation] of 2002, Julia Bolles from the Bolles+Wilson firm of architects states: 'Against the background of the flowing images, it seems to be very radical at the moment to restore a link with physical objects'.[9] This also applies against the background of the increase in scale.

The most striking aspect of Van Breda's article is that it is the teachers, not the managers or the students, who are calling for smallness of scale. In a calculating way the latter appear to have found common ground in their functional view of smallness of scale. Smallness of scale becomes the volatile convergence of like-minded people or congeners – the community of interest – in whose interest it is to form a short-term coalition. Smallness of scale has here been promoted to the rank of Bigness' little helper.

Teachers apparently think differently about it. They see smallness of scale as linked to the basic teaching situation, the communication of knowledge in a classroom situation. In the same week in which that issue of *Schooldomein* appeared, the cinemas were screening the documentary *Être et Avoir* [To be and to have] about a school in the Auvergne run by a single teacher. This fossil-like situation was at the same time an incisive reminder of what makes a school different from a shopping mall. The teacher is not an adviser but someone with authority who communicates knowledge. Smallness of scale is not a temporary coalition, but the creation of a bond of trust. The success of the film in France is undoubtedly connected with the dissatisfaction about the cultural erosion of the French countryside, but the increase of scale in schools in the Netherlands is just as much a form of cultural erosion.

Perhaps smallness of scale is the reflexive moment in this process. That does not imply the start of a revolution, as people still thought in the 1960s. Architects cannot ignore the process of increase of scale any more than the demand for a symbolic architecture on the part of administrators. Still, they can shift the emphasis in the assignment to make the teacher the subject of teaching again and thus more the subject of the architectural commission.

What is typical of the current educational situation is that, besides the teacher as a means of transferring information, there is an enormous quantity of technologically mediated knowledge available too.[10] The subject/object of that knowledge is the quasi-autonomous, shopping and surfing student. The result is a marginalisation of the position of the teacher. From the point of view of the teacher, smallness of scale means that she or he remains in charge on the home front – what used to be called the classroom. This is where students can report on their journeys through all kinds of fields of knowledge and test their experiences against those of the rest. This is where they can talk about both their successes and their failures. The teacher creates the human environment in which individual experiences become shared experiences, where it is not just success that counts, where there is also room for uncertainties and anxieties. This is a crucial part of the learning process.

Seen from the point of view of the architect, smallness of scale has some things in common with the teacher's view, but not all. The emphasis on individual and technologically mediated

learning trajectories has marginalized the school premises.
The limit here is not just learning without a teacher, but also
learning without a school building. In practice a compromise is
sought through flexibility, the buzz word in school architecture
for decades. Flexibility is called upon to reconcile the changing
nature of education with the resistance put up by the building.

Architecture is a medium with two faces. On the one hand,
it forms a part of the technologically mediated world. In large
schools, school life is already run more by monitors than by the
physical space. But architecture is also the medium of accommodation by which we appropriate our surroundings through
our own bodies. That is what adults mention when they talk
about the school premises of their youth. If the school building
is to survive, architects will have to create anchor-points for
this form of knowledge that proceeds through the body. This
can be done by designing from the inside, in a manner that
Adolf Loos propagated in his 'Das Prinzip der Bekleidung' [The
principle of covering].[11] Starting out from the commission, the
architect gropes his or her way towards the spatial design,
imagining the mood that she or he wants to evoke. This image
first takes on specific form in an interaction between space
and covering. The construction only comes afterwards.[12]
Corporeal knowledge of the building may not make monitors
redundant, but it might be able to call a halt to their proliferation.
But it is on the home front that the media alliance of teacher
and architect really wins out over the electronic media. It is here
that something of the fossil teaching situation is brought to life
and that things and people regain their tactile quality. Here the
laptop becomes a piece of furniture whose lid produces a pre-
historic sound when it is clicked shut. *This* smallness of scale
forms an open, indeterminate, poetic element within the large-
scale enterprise.

Notes

1   Syb van Breda, 'Scholen van de toekomst', *Schooldomein* no. 6, July
2003, pp. 30-32.

2   This is based on Jan Drentje, 'Een kenniscultuur bouw je niet snel
weer op', *NRC Handelsblad* 9 July 2003.

3   Royal Haskoning Architecten is an autonomous division of Royal
Haskoning, Consultants, Architects and Engineers.

4   For what follows see Ullrich Schwarz, 'Reflexive Moderne.
Perspektiven der Architektur am Beginn des 21. Jahrhunderts', in:
exh. cat. *Neue Deutsche Architektur -– eine Reflexive Moderne*,
Hatje-Cantz, Ostfildern-Ruit 2003.

5   See Jan Douwe van der Ploeg, *De virtuele boer*, Assen 1999.

6   See Nikolaus Kuhnert and Angelika Schnell, 'Die Moderne der
        Moderne', *ARCH+* no. 143, 1998. The reflexivity of the architecture
        of firms like OMA and MVRDV is supposed to be evident from the
        priority given to the programme, in which form and function are also
        treated as aspects of the programme.
7   The latter qualification is from Andreas Ruby, as cited by Ullrich
        Schwarz in his article.
8   Wouter Deen and Udo Garritzmann, 'Diagrammen van het heden-
        daagse. OMA's little helper op de zoektocht naar het nieuwe',
        Oase no. 48, 1998, pp. 83-93.
9   Julia Bolles-Wilson, 'Ästhetische Globalisierung: Die Bedeutung von
        Kontext in einer virtuellen Welt', lecture delivered at the 'Alpbacher
        Gespräche' held in Alpbach, Austria 2002.
10   Technological mediation is the theme of Petran Kockelkoren. See
        for instance his book 'Technology: Art, Fairground and Theatre',
        Rotterdam 2003.
11   'Das Prinzip der Bekleidung' (1898), in: Adolf Loos, *Ins Leere
        gesprochen*, Georg Prachner, Vienna 1921, pp. 139-146.
12   See too: 'Het lichaam van de architectuur: van antropomorfisme tot
        ergonomie', in: Hilde Heynen et al. (eds), *'Dat is architectuur'.
        Sleutelteksten uit de twintigste eeuw*, Uitgeverij 010, Rotterdam
        2001, pp. 736-746.

Engagement has become everyone's friend

Lucas Verweij and Ton Matton

Is it such a bad thing if involvement is not inspired by noble intentions? Engagement is contemporary, it can be subsidized, and it is politically correct. Engagement has no enemies; everyone supports it. Moreover, a disarming romanticism attaches to it.

Engagement already had a double agenda in the mid-nineteenth century. Better living and working conditions would make people healthier, and thus more productive. Which of the two was the 'real' goal remains unanswered. If, at that time, engagement was still the concern of a few exceptional individuals, then since the introduction of the 1901 Housing Act that marked the dawn of social housing policy in the Netherlands, an unending stream of engagement has coursed through the twentieth century: the Rent Control Act, pension provisions, medical care, suffrage, sheltered housing for the elderly, the Bijlmermeer modernist urban expansion of the 1960s, the 'Van Dam unit' named after the advocate of studio-type housing in the 1970s, the Bauhaus, the Van Nelle factory, Rietveld and Wassily chairs, and so on.

This engagement was often inspired by a conjunction of social (i.e. left-leaning) politics and committed designers, as with Plan Zuid and the Bijlmermeer, for example. Sometimes it was spawned by an enlightened commissioner and a designer, as with the Van Nelle factory and Rietveld's Red and Blue Chair. For a century, engagement has been the fountainhead of practically all noteworthy developments in the field of design. However, designers have nearly always relied on other people in order to render projects on a larger scale, to make them more comprehensive or more meaningful and better thought out.

Institutional

Engagement has now penetrated into every facet of society. It is a fixed component in diverse government bodies, in associations, foundations, political parties and subsidy providers. Urban renewal, public safety policy and the Dutch government's 'Postbus 51' central information services are all semi-institutionalized forms of engagement that flowed from a process of engagement's social embedding. In order to allow that process of embedding to proceed smoothly, engagement has been reduced to manageable proportions in clearly defined projects with measurable objectives. Nowhere is engagement as accessible and manageable as here in the Netherlands, where there is a long tradition of institutionalized engagement.

As the role of architects in the actual construction process was gradually stepped back during the 1980s and '90s, the personal involvement of the architects became less relevant. The engagement is covered by the project remit and building legislation, as set out by the team of commissioners, developers, municipal departments, groups of residents and the like. There is no architect who can sidestep the building standards, and his or her political preferences or possible engagement no longer matters. In the Netherlands you can realize engaged projects with brutes as designers.

Suspect

Engagement in relation to design is often – if not always – suspect. While for the utopians it was already not exclusively a matter of the health of workers but certainly also about higher industrial productivity, nowadays engagement certainly contributes to higher turnover. The industrial giants do their very best to create an engaged brand identity. Besides its inhuman oil extraction in Nigeria, Shell now produces 'cleaner' energy, and it has involved large sections of society in its ethical dilemmas since the Brent Spar disaster. From then on, we have all become co-decision-makers in Shell's problems. It is hardly likely that this engagement has arisen spontaneously, instead being consciously stage-managed by Shell's advertising bureau after the boycott in connection with the apartheid regime in South Africa. The disengaged stance of the multinational began to have a negative impact on turnover, so something had to be done. The communications strategists have done their job superbly: Shell is no longer the immoral bogeyman, but a responsible concern which shares its worldly problems with us openly. They have even appointed an in-house ethicist to advise them.

Another exemplary giant, McDonald's, cuts down forests in order to provide grazing for its hamburger cattle, yet it showily recycles its mountains of waste and rubbish, witness the juggernauts etched on everyone's mind because they are so carefully designed. The multinational also pays a great deal of attention to communicating the message that eating hamburgers is healthy and that the resulting trash cannot be all that harmful. As the icing on the cake, there is Ronald McDonald: the clown who leads an exemplary independent life, managed by foundations at a safe arm's length from the mother concern. He was

even responsible for top-notch architecture here in the Netherlands, in the form of the Ronald McDonald houses designed by
Claus en Kaan and Bosch Hasslett.

Yet engagement is not only an instrument at two removes
for the bigger corporations. Engagement is also a beloved
theme of individual designers. The engagement is exaggerated,
but it is often primarily a media game of 'self-branding', drawing
attention to oneself as a brand. In the recent 'Neau thirst' project
(tap water that was sold in bottles for the price of mineral
water, with profits going to developing countries), the design
bureau (Vandejong) got star billing as author and initiator, in a
big, hip typeface and with an explanation of the link with their
corporate identity. It cuts both ways.

Here too, the question is whether engagement is about
active involvement, or whether the designers are simply doing
their job and coincidentally work on engaged design briefs. The
fact is that engagement is the Achilles heel of the baby-boom
generation that currently holds the reins. They like to see
engagement in projects, which means it has become a successful design theme. It is, after all, 'marketable'. Consider the work
of architects like Mecanoo, MVRDV and Liesbeth van der Pol
or, in the visual arts, Alicia Framis, Bureau Venhuizen and B.a.d
Enterprises. The work of our own bureau, Schie 2.0, could also
be viewed in this same light.

Thanks to the realization of democratic goals in architecture, as well as the sharing of power, it is likely that social
and political engagement were more at home in the last century
than in the current one. Other grandiose themes will gradually
steer and eventually define architecture and design. What then
are those themes?

Leisure-time engagement

A derivative of social engagement is marginal engagement.
This development is gradually evolving into a new theme in
architecture. People are prepared to engage with their own
social class. Rather than being based on a philosophy of life or
a religious belief, this new pillarization is built up in strata that
are determined by social status and financial means. Examples
include the downgrading of student grants to student loans
which students have to repay later out of their own pockets,
the old-age pension debate prompted by today's taxpayers no
longer wanting to support pensioners, and a housing market
where access to the lowest rung of the property ladder is
restricted because you can only get a mortgage with a permanent job. In the Vinex urban expansion schemes there is no

longer even a hint of an evenly balanced demographic, with building programmes unambiguously targeting the middle classes. Social housing projects no longer embrace a mingling of old people, junkies and the poor, but the addition of facilities to one's private dwelling instead; a jointly run vegetarian restaurant, a communal garden, sauna or nursery – amenities which are used by similar sections of the population (middle-aged working people). The engagement that underlies this could be termed 'leisure-time engagement'. Hobbies are starting to determine the character of the living environment: a residential block with a shared car, a community based around rearing free-range chickens, tending an apple orchard or growing organic vegetables, special housing for people allergic to house-dust mites, or a communal satellite dish for global TV reception.

Safe-haven engagement

Safety could become an important theme, not with the goal of making society a less hostile place, but because of the wish to own and properly protect one's own property: barred windows, road barriers, private security services and alarm installations. The securely guarded condominium is the urban model in Sao Paulo. Engagement exists within the safe confines of house and car, and is reserved for the individual who is granted access. The social engagement is zero and therefore the mistrust of everything that is not privately protected is enormous. The public space can be done away with because it represents nothing but a lack of safety; life only exists in isolated capsules. This ego-engagement extends no further than family and friends. Everything revolves around the individual and his or her property. The property-less, as is the case today, play no role of consequence in architecture. With ego-engagement, the private commissioner and his or her degree of fear sets the programme for the architect.

I-engagement

Due to the directness of the mass media, processes which initially applied exclusively to entertainment have now wafted over to the design world. Designers make their careers via and thanks to the media. With the hundreds of periodicals – professional and consumer-oriented – newspapers, debates and the like, the personality of the designer plays an ever-greater role. We must seriously consider whether we designers should take media training courses as a component of our studies, courses on which they teach people how to come across pleasantly on the radio, how to turn out statements that provide good material for quotes, and how to respond with snappy and astute answers. The discipline might even be expanded to include personality development: how to walk, how to talk, how to come across as a solid personality.

It might sound funny, but it is serious – one of the big developments in design and in terms of importance comparable with the engagement in the last century, could well turn out to be stardom. Designers could soon depend more on their communication and social skills than on their design skills. For politicians, football referees, business executives, judges, interviewers and other high-profile figures, this is already the case in their everyday business, and it is not improbable that designers will soon rank alongside them. A portrait of the designer accompanies articles about design work more and more often, and it is fair to assume that the photo sessions will get longer and the interviews shorter.

The lenient house

On the betrothal of house and home

1

'Painted ladies' is what they are called, the Victorian houses of San Francisco. And indeed, they have dolled themselves up lavishly, colourfully and initially with lots of frills, like ladies aiming to face the world in a light and defiant way.

Many of these frills, like the ornate wood carving along the eaves, were eroded away in the course of time by the stiff breeze of maintenance costs. Also the stained glass disappeared, as did the moneyed middle class living there. The houses fell into disrepair until, just in the nick of time, they were rediscovered in the 1970s, often by the gay community which in these years started to secure itself a visible place in the city. The 'painted ladies' offered lots of space for what was then little money, and so with pots of paints and flower-boxes gentrification started.

The ladies' ground plan is less well-known than their exuberant façades. It is largely always the same, straightforward and rather dull to the connoisseur. 'An absolutely generic space plan', Stewart Brand calls it in his book *How Buildings Learn*. Between three and six 'through-rooms' are found in a row, interconnected by sliding doors, with a broad corridor alongside of them and an extension at the back, and all this is repeated upstairs again.

In other words, these houses are standardized boxes in timber-frame construction, merely painted and dolled up differently each time. Yet their ground plan is the real secret about them. Also in this case true, abiding beauty is found within.

You could not call these houses neutral. For all their ostentation, they certainly had to attest to a sound, respectable and in every way successful family life. The parents received their guests downstairs in the parlour or library, upstairs the children slept their well-earned sleep, while the servants buzzed busily in the basement. There was room for three or even four generations. Life was spacious, generous and went like clockwork.

Long gone are the social structure and customs of living of that era, but the houses have survived. They are smooth changers, easily adapted to new residents, offering room for new kinds of households, new ways of living, new life styles and new layouts. These family homes can be converted into a boarding house, an office, a number of student flats, subdivided per floor or per half a floor, and usually all this is quite reversible to boot.

That is because all rooms are more or less similar in size (about four by four metres), because it is possible to combine them or keep them separate, and particularly because of the hallway spanning the entire depth of the house, two metres wide and thus capacious enough for all kinds of temporary or permanent additions, like toilets, showers and closets.

All this is chiefly due to the hallway. Here, the name 'circulation space' is inadequate, for it is a hallway like a *turning basin*. Anne Vernez Moudon, who carefully carried out an internal examination of the painted ladies, is quoted in *How Buildings Learn*: 'Thus the hall, which diagrammatically appears like mere circulation space, becomes the support core that relieves the rest of the box from clutter. The generous width of the hall is also the major reason for the inherent flexibility of the box.'

2

Moudon's book *Built for Change* appeared in 1986. Four years later, visual artist Sohela Farokhi and architect Lars Lerup designed a new 'Victorian' residential building, as part of the exhibition 'Visionary San Francisco' at the local Museum of Modern Art.

The plan of their 'House of Flats' is amazing, for it is both obvious and irresistible. Four identical rooms are situated one behind the other along a wide, long corridor, all separated from one another by a small room or antechamber. Thus a chain arises of larger and smaller rooms that can be adjoined and disconnected by way of no less than six sliding doors.

The storey can be used as a regular three or four-roomed flat, with a living room, master bedroom and bedroom for the children. Also two people can live here either together or semi-independently, each occupying two rooms. A combination of business and living is possible too, or for instance student flats with the four rooms being used separately, while a large family or a commune can take an extra floor. And just add a lift and the house will serve you a lifetime.

The size of the rooms and anterooms (around four by three and one by three metres in the plan) may vary, as may the number of floors and the width of the windows and sliding doors. Farokhi and Lerup provided their design with bays jutting out far at the street front, a continuation of Victorian exorbitance by other means. In order to let enough light into the rooms, a strip of garden has been kept clear next to the building, which obviously makes the House of Flats a first cousin of the 'slatted house' in the Amsterdam quarter Borneo-Sporenburg, the way architect Adriaan Geuze in fact intended it.

It is, in short, an attempt to expressly incorporate the qualities which the Victorian box showed almost accidentally and in retrospect, and to elaborate on them. But it is more than that, as appears from the book coming with the exhibition 'Visionary San Francisco'.

The House of Flats is attended by an essay by the writer Richard Rodriguez, which opens with the irony of the housing market seeing to it 'that gay men found themselves living within the architectural metaphor for family'. The family home brought back memories of the sexual secret that had to remain concealed, nowhere more anxiously so than at home, and by now living one's own life within such an edifice these spectres had also been dispelled.

Just at the time when the interior decorator was miraculously styling the apartments into little private 'castles' after they had been split up, history took a new turn with the outbreak of AIDS. And this caused a different story to force its way into the essay that started off so proudly with the Victorian ladies' new life, to wit the drama of a new death. Rodriguez informs us that he has placed a 19th-century mirror over his fireplace recently, from the estate of one of the deceased. He sits in his room as the 'inheritor of the empty mirror'.

What the essay and the design have in common is an awareness of seriousness. To live one's life in a house – to make use of it, settle and reside in it, sharing an existence and a dwelling – may very well be light and defiant and colourful and ornate, but it is also a serious matter. It is a political question in the broadest sense of the word, and perhaps a moral one as well.

And that is why Farokhi and Lerup balance their plan on the sharp edge of a double critique. Their ground plan goes against the 'inscription of the single family in the traditional plan', but likewise against the total rejection of this type in more recent building. Behind the ideological content and manner of use – being products of their time –, they are seeking a classic ground plan.

'Consequently, our House of Flats attempts to erase the "family" from the plan while simultaneously utilizing the tremendous typological power of the Victorian house. The result is, in our mind, an excavation of the type, revealing an underlying stratum, a more fundamental plan if you will.'

3

Have you noticed how little has been said up to now about the architect? The Victorian box does not seem to be in need of one. Instead of innovation, the designers of the House of Flats personally emphasize the excavation of an archetype. At stories about life unfolding within a house, it befits the planner to step back; here, there is nothing for him to draw or direct.

Between architecture and the way it is used an uneasy relationship exists. Stereotypically, residents complain about unpractical planning, and among architects there is a certain wariness of, as Stewart Brand puts it, 'the traumatic instant of letting users into a building'.

Even though this is a caricature, the uneasiness is genuine. Clare Cooper Marcus – architect and landscape gardener, also in San Francisco – writes about this at the beginning of her book *House as a Mirror of Self*. For years, she has been doing surveys into housing preferences, but she is still not very sure what living in a house really means and writes: 'I was learning and communicating a lot about *house* (kitchen design, room layout, privacy needs, inadequate storage, and so on), but little about *home*. During my early years as a graduate student and young faculty member at Berkeley, I moved ten times in ten years. Each time, the actual physical move was followed by weeks, sometimes months, of getting used to the new place. (...) I reflected on my own feelings about moving and settling into a new place and realized that my door-to-door surveys in housing projects were only skimming the surface of what house and home mean to the human heart.'

In order to penetrate the surface of house and home, she used the work of the psychoanalyst Carl Jung. From it, she derived the image of the interactive mirror: the mirror that shows me who I am, but I can also change myself by looking into it. Apart from this, Jung is interesting as he built a house himself, worked on it for more than thirty years and interpreted every alteration in relation to his own emotional development.

Also Marcus' Canadian colleague Witold Rybczynski is, at the beginning of *Home*, astonished by the blind spot between the architect's profession and a house's everyday use. This time the angle is not the psyche but comfort: 'During the six years of my architectural education the subject of comfort was mentioned only once. It was by a mechanical engineer whose job it was to initiate my classmates and me into the mysteries of air conditioning and heating. (...) It was a curious omission from an otherwise rigorous curriculum; one would have thought that comfort was a crucial issue in preparing for the architectural profession, like justice in law, or health in medicine.'

The uneasiness between design and the way it is utilized finds heightened expression when an architect plans a house for personal use. Here, there is tremendous dedication, the out-

come is occasionally unusual, but many a marriage has suc-
cumbed along the way. That is why an architect may also choose
to take a different line which somewhat resembles a survival
strategy. As one architect told me recently: 'One doesn't want
too much architecture in one's own home.'

4

The tackling of this uneasy relationship between design and the
way it is used requires a special kind of commitment. Not a
commitment of big words, full of romantic idealism and provoca-
tive, but a rather more diminutive, more pedestrian commitment,
attentive and unobtrusive at the same time. For this homely
commitment, *betrothal* – an expression of commitment – is a
suitable metaphor.

Betrothal or getting engaged is generally regarded as the
most unexciting link in the chain 'in love-engaged-married'. It
lacks the euphoric peak experience of being in love and also the
staggering perspective of faithfulness for ever. Yet it does seek
to combine these two extremes: the ideal engagement is loving,
but also somewhat reserved and formal. That sounds like a
good recipe for the betrothal of architecture and everyday life.

This engagement needs room to manoeuvre. With reference
to Dutch ecclesiastical history, it argues in favour of striving for
a 'lenient' instead of a 'strict' architecture. To refresh your
memory: the Strict were the Dutch orthodox Calvinists during
the sixteenth century, while their latitudinarian contemporaries
were called Lenients or Moderates.

A 'strict' building resembles a made-to-measure suit, fitting
like a glove. It meets its requirements of use very precisely. And
of course there are admirable strict buildings, dictating their
utilization forcefully and authoritatively. But even the best
made-to-measure suit has this one disadvantage: that when the
body in it grows or shrinks, the suit no longer has a good fit.
Moreover, a lot of housing is often merely a vague attempt at
made-to-measure, in which the measurements are not taken
from the initial and subsequent residents, but from legal and
commercial standards. That is why it does not fit well and is
simply too tight.

A lenient building is also planned with a specific way of
use in mind, and just like the strict building it can be the
expression of a view of life, of social values or an idea as to the
way of living in a house. But instead of fitting closely, its use is
surrounded by a buffer of indefiniteness. A lenient house is
magnanimous towards the life that will go on in it and tolerant
of deviations. You need not know or decide everything concern-

ing its future use right away. The 'painted ladies' of San Francisco are outstanding examples of lenient buildings.

Also the Netherlands has its lenient buildings, in which life is able to unfold with a certain ease. A Dutch canal house is a lenient building and part of the nineteenth-century housing stock is too. Also the middleclass homes from the thirties are lenient, split up into 'through-rooms' interconnected by sliding doors (called rooms *en suite* in Dutch), a form which twenty years later was diligently modernized into oblivion. Also under the auspices of council housing, lenient houses arose, like – to mention two examples from the eighties – the 'sliding-door dwellings' by Margreet Duinker and Machiel van der Torre in the Amsterdam Dapperbuurt district, and the homes by Alvaro Siza in the Schilderswijk of The Hague.

And still such spacious, lenient houses are being built. The ARCAM paperback *Formats for Living* includes even something that is almost a painted lady, designed by Tangram, of which the commentator Liesbeth van der Pol writes: 'The design (...) is a very old-fashioned "through-room" dwelling, but it looks very comfortable, everything is in its place. In effect, it is a nineteenth-century floor plan, simplified, well organized and attractive; it radiates tranquillity.' Here, the antithesis in the words 'old-fashioned *but* comfortable' is striking.

Yet there are exceptions. The inventiveness of Dutch architects is often engaged in a very different fight, to wit the Houdini-like struggle within the web of regulations and conditions. Thus heroic feats have been performed on the narrow, deep lots of Borneo-Sporenburg in order to see to it that all of the rooms have their legally required portion of sun. Apart from this, many houses mainly derive their character from their appearance, from branding or from town-planning arrangements. However spectacular they may look, under their 'skin' there usually lurks a respectable but unremarkable ground plan. New housing in 'thirties style' imitates superficial style features, but seldom offers the space, the rooms *en suite* and the storey height of the genuine thirties' edifices.

Then there remains the great bulk of mediocre new housing estates of which an inventory was made by A. Straub, at least as regards the period up to 1998, in *Woningontwerp op Vinex-locaties* (*Housing design on Vinex sites*, i.e. government-allocated sites for urban expansion), a report that deserves a sequel and more widespread attention. One is not cheered by this outline. All this is the epitome of *off-the-peg*: 'At the front of the house, no space remains for the living room, as this is taken up by the entrance.' 'The hall is usually cramped.' 'Although a favourite with the buyers, the separate kitchen is only found in 5% of the plans scrutinized.' 'The children's bedrooms are often small; 6 m^2 is no exception. It is doubtful whether these rooms can serve the intended purpose, or any other purpose for that matter.' 'Facilities to simply combine two tiny bedrooms into a larger space (...) are lacking everywhere.' 'The number of dwellings offering the possibility to live in them in different ways than follows logically from their plan, is very small indeed.'

Even the developers and real-estate agents selling them acknowledge that *Vinex* houses will at the most give short-term satisfaction: 'The developers admit that the products they are offering today (...) are not the houses that are going to meet the future demand.'

5

The lenient house is not a complicated edifice to understand or to build, and once it is there it is popular. Still, in practice, it proves extremely difficult to realize.

How is this possible? In part it is due to the fact that architects are hired – engaged – by others than the prospective occupants, people with different priorities and different interests. Architects and users are in a certain sense companions in adversity; they find themselves at either end of a far too long and complicated chain of go-betweens.

And, apart from this, it is due to the fact that a lenient house is a building for the long term, as leniency does not pay off straight away. This clashes with the financial logic as to building homes, in which the write-off period tends to shrink more and more, as if houses were cars or fridges.

So something will have to be thought up to shorten the chain and shatter the logic of rigid exploitation. Occasionally this can be done in a direct way when a house is commissioned by a private client. But apart from that, also the lenient house will have to be reconsidered, planned, discussed and taken seriously again, as an opportunity for a conspiracy of designers and users. The tradition of ground-plan innovation may receive a new boost, this time by taking as its guiding principle not Houdinian ingenuity, but Victorian magnanimity.

With a view to this, we ought to phrase *requirements of leniency*. These will have to be programmatic, but over and above this the programme should include requirements as to indulgence. Here is an example, more or less phrased off the cuff: one may expect of a house that one is able to live in it in different manners without all too much discomfort. One must be able to change the way in which a house is used, or rather it should remain usable under altered circumstances, like a room gradually evolving from nursery to teenage den. There should be no great dissimilarity as regards room size, unless this can be corrected simply and pliantly. A room must be able to contain various degrees of spatial and functional discretion, of openness and seclusion, of public and private. You ought to be able to receive visitors there, friends acting as if they were at home as well as guests within a more formal setting. Part of the requirement of discretion is also that a workroom like the kitchen does not unavoidably impose itself upon the guests. A kitchen need not necessarily be at the front of the house, and a living room should not at all costs face away from the street. The hallway will have to be large enough to allow an overcoat to be donned and doffed without discomfort of movement.

These requirements are not neutral; they presuppose a life of which the public part is not strictly kept outside of the home. Neither are they absolute requirements. Not every house will have to meet them. Still, a designer will need to keep them at the back of his mind, as requirements of leniency. These are tolerance requirements, stimulating a certain way of living in a house, without excluding all too many other uses. The benefits lie in its everyday use and also in its durability, during a long future in which the occupants can change without moving and the house can change without having to be replaced.

Inspiration may be found in well-tried typologies that have a high degree of leniency, like the rooms *en suite*. Such a suite of rooms segments the space and offers the double spatial experience in which you simultaneously find yourself within a small and a larger room. Rooms *en suite* are functional and facilitate degrees of proximity and distance. They even offer 'theatrical' possibilities – because staging home performances between the sliding doors used to be a proverbial Dutch pastime. Also, they make it possible, whenever necessary and for as long as one wishes, to differentiate between formal and informal space. This means that the deacon or the insurance agent can be received in the front room, with the sliding doors closed, as there is no need for the man to go wandering about the entire house.

Rooms *en suite* represent freedom of choice. They can be opened and shut, they can constitute either a single large room or two smaller ones, it is all possible and yet one is not compelled to choose. Ever since they have disappeared from the standard repertoire of building, the choice has become poorer. What objection could there be to bringing them back?

The lenient house can also benefit from old as well as new concepts for support and infill. As to this, you should first and foremost direct your design effort towards a support that is spacious as a turning basin, while the infill activity can remain slight and unobtrusive. Perhaps it should not be a dual concept (support and infill) but a triple one, analogous to the strata theory in environmental planning.

Furthermore, Anne Vernez Moudon's suggestion to take the *room* instead of the *house* as the basic unit in housing design deserves elaboration. 'A return to the room as module for residential design is a necessary step toward creating resilient space. We must abandon the use of *dwellings* as modules of spatial organization.'

The lenient house, as an expression of tolerance and as a practical frame for a long and mobile life, is perhaps not the highest ideal imaginable, but it can offer common ground for both architecture and the manners a home is lived in. It promises a betrothal of *house* and *home*, and that is no small commitment.

Literature

Stewart Brand, *How Buildings Learn. What Happens After They're Built*, Phoenix Illustrated, London 1997 (first publ. 1994).
Clare Cooper Marcus, *House as a Mirror of Self. Exploring the Deeper Meaning of Home*,
Maarten Kloos, Dave Wendt (eds.), *Formats for Living; Contemporary floor plans in Amsterdam*, ARCAM/Architectura & Natura Press, Amsterdam 2000.
Anne Vernez Moudon, *Built for Change. Neighborhood Architecture in San Francisco*, MIT Press, Cambridge (Mass.) 1986.
Paolo Polledri (ed.), *Visionary San Francisco*, Prestel, Munich 1990
Witold Rybczynski, *Home; A Short History of an Idea*, Penguin Books, New York 1987 (first publ. 1986).
A. Straub (et al), *Woningontwerp op Vinex-locaties* (Bouwmanagement en Technisch Beheer 19), Delft University Press, Delft 1999.

Engagement is perfectly ordinary

Allard Jolles

'Architecture's task is no easier than that in other social fields where people do not identify with the status quo, which is to say with the discrepancy between spectacular technological progress and the archaization of human relations.'

The above quotation would appear to be about the current disparity between the tumultuous ICT developments taking place in the design discipline and the 'norms and values' debate initiated by various European politicians and referred to here as 'the archaization of human relations'. Nothing could be further from the truth. This text dates from 1966 and was written by the German psychologist Klaus Horn. The dilemma it describes relates to the age-old 'form follows function' equation, into which Horn very much wanted to see the 'human' element inserted. The 'spectacular technological progress' in Horn's case is the standardization of housing construction, and the 'archaization of human relations' refers to the already present longing for an old-fashioned, cosy village atmosphere. For that was sorely lacking in all those wonderful, large-scale, high-rise housing estates. Horn's argument is included in an anthology devoted to architecture and ideology. An engaged designer, the writers included in that anthology all agree, takes care to produce an architectural and urban design of such quality that individuals will, in spite of everything, be able to feel at home in those modern, technologically dynamic surroundings.

How is that sense of being at home, that yearning for security, nowadays? And what, if anything, does it have to do with engagement? Broadly speaking, designers adopt one of two strategies. The one is that of concealment: Rob Krier is someone who is good at that. Inside, his buildings are identical to all other modern residential buildings but he masks this with a coating of varnish from earlier times. The other strategy consists of flaunting all the technical gadgets along with the sales argument 'equipped with all mod cons'. Technology is there for you, exclaims the brochure, whereupon the tangle of cables, the forest of steel and the vast expanses of glass actually start to look more benign. Thus, the homebuyer either gets a mask of conviviality or an Internet connection and a home page sporting the name of the new suburb sandwiched between 'www' and '.nl'. Hybrid forms of these strategies, such as the excessively cabled upmarket semi, are also on the increase.

But where is the human element in these strategies? Regrettably, the end-users often only come into view when the houses have to be sold or when the street is officially opened. This is directly related to the lack of social involvement among architects and urban designers that observers have been calling attention to for some time now. Do designers still actually think about the end-user? Too little, alas, and that lack of interest starts during the design work, which nowadays leans heavily on the capabilities of the latest software. In essence, every new plan is made with Microsoft. Which is why every new-build project looks like every other new-build project, apart from the facade sauce. But the most important thing, of course, is that every manifestation of architecture or urban design, every building and every street in other words, is aimed at human beings and is thus 'intensely human'. However much use is made of software, the design discipline is essentially unchanged: it begins with a good idea. The Dutch critic Max Bruinsma is referring to the same thing when he quotes ICT specialist Caroline Nevejan in his essay 'The Future as Artwork': 'It is not ICT that moves or touches, it is the interaction between artist and pubic that makes something happen...'. Like Horn 35 years earlier, Bruinsma in his essay is looking for the individual caught between form and function. He notes that the manifestations of the various media are becoming increasingly individualized. Indeed, it is quite a simple matter nowadays to make something unique, for a single person, the best example to date being the customized newspaper purged of all the items we do not wish to read. Added to which, place and space are less important in the digital age. When you look at a painting – the *Mona Lisa*, for example – in a museum, the simple fact that you are standing right in front of the 'real deal' affects your experience. But nowadays, wherever you are, the computer enables you to step into every painting. As a consequence, time is much more important and the art experience probably just as intense, even if it is 'not real'. Physical presence has made way for a temporary connectivity. Time makes everything real.

Thus, and this is borne out by the above, recent technological developments have not made it impossible to create anything unique. As far as that is concerned, there is no need for the individual to be submerged in the collective. But why do we notice so little of this in current design practice?

In 1935, Walter Benjamin wrote 'The Work of Art in the Age of Mechanical Reproduction'. Benjamin's idea has long since been stood on its head: reproduction *is* today's artwork. And nobody is more aware of this than architects and urban designers now that more and more commissions are the same and they are asked time and again to repeat themselves: a redesign of a shopping street, a research park along the A such and such, one more urban expansion scheme, or another attention-getting museum in a city in want of a logo. If we couple the notion of reproduction to the previously observed importance of time nowadays, architecture and urban design should actually have little cause for worry. For what two disciplines are better at incorporating (copy/paste) time into their 'artwork'? After all, it is 'space, *time* and architecture' isn't it? And what disciplines are better at copying and recycling their own work, something that used to be very chicly known as an 'a personal style'? The problem is that all that clever software makes it absurdly easy to devise a 'new' design; all it takes are a few clicks of the mouse. What designer could resist? The latest housing scheme is often no more than a digital mutant of its immediate predecessor. And it's successful, too. The local Dutch culture has become such a readily reproducible product that it seems as if the target group was not the *locals* but the *globals*. Nor is this confined to the design discipline. *Big Brother*'s recent international coup could never have been pulled off by the makers of that Dutch 1960s children's television hit *Swiebertje*.

Let's return for a moment to the 1960s, where Swiebertje's and Klaus Horn's contemporaries are busy designing the Bijlmermeer housing estate in Amsterdam. Thousands of dwellings, in repetitive rows, in flats that are in turn all identical and grouped together in a pattern. It sounds like an early version of reproducibility as artwork. But nothing could be less true. This plan is primarily about the collective–individual relationship, about 'we live here' versus 'I live here'. But the happiness of the individual is the true subject of the plan. Street level, for example, belongs to us, pedestrian or cyclist, and all that 'dangerous traffic' has its own level. The style or signature of the designer is absolutely of secondary importance. That is the kind of engagement Horn so warmly advocates. The designers back then did not see it like that, they simply did their work, and as well as possible. They used reproducibility as a means, not as an end or as artwork. And they did so without any guarantee of a favourable outcome, for the success of a plan depends just as much on chance and actual use, as on the quality of the design. The history of the Bijlmer has certainly taught us that.

And yet ... 'simply doing one's work' forms the basis for renewed engagement in architecture and urban design. And the next step is that designers should not boast too much about this. For when the desire to stand in the spotlight is father to the design, engagement does not get much of look in.

On everyday engagement

Arnold Reijndorp

Mr Reijndorp, you belonged to a small group of students who 'reached out into the neighbourhoods' to support the residents in 'their struggle for better living conditions', following the democratization of the Faculty of Architecture in Delft. You may well have studied architecture, but you graduated – together with a small group again – with a project titled 'Towards a socialist urban politics', which one could only call 'architecture' with a considerable stretch of the imagination. After graduating, you worked for the project team that coordinated the urban renewal in the Oude Westen ('Old West') quarter of Rotterdam, 'building for the neighbourhood' as it was known then. Then you worked for an inter-university research institute with the remarkable name 'Institute for norms and values in industrial society', which had already been tainted by the democratization movement, too, and primarily pursued 'active research'. Following the closure of that institute, you ended up at the University of Amsterdam, where you lectured on urban sociology and pursued research into the social and cultural changes in various older city neighbourhoods. In your free time you also worked with Links Rotterdam, a left-wing coalition of the CPN (the Dutch Communist Party), PPR ('Political Party Radicals') and PSP ('Pacifist Socialist Party'), and represented them on Rotterdam City Council for a short time. You also served on the board of a neighbourhood development company, a foundation offering support for drug addicts, and a health centre in a 'deprived neighbourhood'. For the last 10 years or so, you have been working as an independent researcher and you are still obstinately striving to bridge the gap between 'the social' and 'the physical-spatial'. You call yourself an 'errand-boy between sociology and urban planning'. Mr Reijndorp, what does engagement mean in architecture and urban planning?

Rietveld! There is a film about Rietveld – I saw it a few years ago at an exhibition of his work in Antwerp. You see him – a friendly, somewhat plain fellow, filmed from a low angle while he explains what he does – folding a small piece of paper into a minuscule chair. If you see him absorbed like this, then you cannot help but think that it is as simple as that. At the same time, you know that there is a story behind it. You know the story behind De Stijl as well, or, if you do not, then the didactic approach of a presentation like this imprints it on your mind. It is also a tale about engagement, about resistance to the vulgarity of mass production, about new beauty, new 'imaging', purity and simplicity. Yet that whole story only fits into place on seeing that simple act of folding that little chair. You notice that the history of De Stijl is a highly personal story for Rietveld, much sooner professionally inspired than ideologically or politically. It addresses the essence of architecture and arts and crafts in an era of mass production, and the emancipation of the working class, but it is primarily about making things; and while these things are not devoid of meaning, they are certainly lacking in pretension.

Rietveld endeavoured to create something that spoke for itself. The revolutionary aspect of his designs – certainly for the time – is a superficially contradictory yet completely natural product of a highly restrained notion of how to make things. His was a philosophy which is almost apologetic for what the creation of something novel simultaneously alters or destroys, the place that the new thing occupies, the space that it fills, the materials it has consumed, and the attention it demands. The new thing tries to compensate that loss by giving back something that people perceive as an enrichment, as if it were something that was always there or, rather, as something that should have been there all the time. The loss is thus transposed into the resolution of a deficiency.

I once had the honour of accompanying Henk Engel and Jan de Heer to an interview with Mrs Schröder-Schräder, who was then still living in the Rietveld-Schröder House. That was an occasion to remember. She talked about Rietveld's fondness for a nice piece of wood. He would suddenly walk in with an oak table leaf with a wonderful drawing. After a short while it would disappear under a plain tablecloth, and would subsequently be removed from the house altogether. It demanded too much attention, took up too much space. Rietveld's restrained design philosophy resulted in practical discomforts, but these are irrelevant in the light of the recurring spatial experiences at every turn. Every winter, like clockwork, the diagonal window in the 'living room' would be the source of a mound of snow on the floor. However, opening the window, Mrs Schröder-Schräder exclaimed, 'Just look at that, how wonderful! That makes it worth it.' That is indeed so.

I cannot count the discussions I have had with sociology students who thought Rem Koolhaas was a bad architect because his buildings leaked. I do not want to go so far as to say that a building is only good architecture if it leaks, but there is something to it. Sometimes it is impossible to do justice to all the properties of an object in equal portion. Rietveld made a window that in the first place 'imaged' the space in a new way, a window that primarily opened up the room to the outside, primarily intended to be opened at the first hint of spring. Does such a window have to leak when it is closed? No, not necessarily – we learnt that much even in Delft, but all the same …. If such a window does not leak, then you do indeed get the feeling that less would have been more, something lighter, more modest. Paradoxically enough, these practical imperfections are the flipside of a design philosophy that strove to be self-evident, which is not quite the same thing as lacking in depth. It is a striving for perfection, without wanting to be perfect in everything.

The things that Rietveld made were not intended to make something obvious to us. They do not strive to be anything more than what they actually are: a window that opens up the space, a chair that you can sit on. They do not aim to make any statements about the quintessence of the window or the chair; they are, however, about the essence of making something, about the technology and the method of production.

Things do not need to have meanings attached to them in order to be meaningful. Bruno Latour, a French sociologist who focuses especially on 'things', explains this using an unusual Berlin key.[1] It is a remarkable object, with a bit at both ends, specially designed for the entrances to the apartment buildings that were built en masse in Berlin around the turn of the nineteenth century. A modern-day visitor who wants to open the door with one of these keys is confronted with an irritating problem: if the lock is opened, it is impossible to get the key out. You can turn the key to lock the door again and then withdraw the key, but then you are back to where you started. If you are lucky, a resident will come home before too long, and demonstrate how the key works: you stick it in the lock, turn it to open the lock and push it through the keyhole to the inside, then you open the door and, once inside, you lock the door again and only then can you remove the key.

You could, of course, attach all kinds of meanings to this key, Latour notes. You might, for example, use it to illustrate the functioning of a microphysics of power à la Foucault, or as a disciplining strategy as proposed by Elias. However, perhaps the meaning simply rests in the solution that the key offers for a complex social problem. This problem is inherent to this new form of urban living, the relatively anonymous commune of relative strangers. This remarkable object prevents much of the social friction that is expressed in the posting of notices with texts like 'Please close the door after you', or the less friendly 'Shut the door!'

Things can free us from moral dilemmas, as with the tourniquets of the metro which remind us that we must buy a ticket and the electronic gates in shop doorways which gently dissuade us from stealing the objects of our desire. They do this without respect of persons. It is of no consequence to these things whether we are male or female, rich or poor, white or black, familiar or unknown, chic or shabby. That is what distinguishes them from the doorman, the caretaker and the security guard.

Perhaps we could make the same demands of architecture and urbanism: do not saddle us with moral issues, but give us the conditions to deal with them. The debate about urbanism and spatial planning is dominated by moral claims. On reading policy documents about the encouragement of urban living and mixed neighbourhoods, one gets the impression that in fact nobody would want to live like that. Everyone who can afford it wants to live in the country, preferably on a private plot and certainly not with other groups – the less fortunate or foreigners – in one and the same neighbourhood. And most certainly not with people who do not quite fit in or who have a screw loose.

The spatial policy gives the impression of being a necessary counterbalance to developments driven by individualism, consumerism and self-interest, fear for everything that is foreign, which work towards the disintegration of society. The spatial planning policy constitutes 'resistance' and that is a demand which architecture and urbanism are increasingly expected to satisfy. Architecture critics criticize the lack of resistance of an architecture that too easily goes along with the urge for distinction among a growing middle class of consumers. This reduces architecture to an accessory for the representation of lifestyles, whether that fits with a brand that is stamped on a particular neighbourhood or not. This criticism is certainly not unfounded. It is unclear, however, where the resistance or resilience that is demanded of architecture can find 'anchoring points' in the midst of societal developments that tend in another direction. Without these points of application, the requirement may well be morally high-minded, but it is a false call to social engagement. Architecture and urbanism are then embedded in a pedagogical project aimed at citizenship and social solidarity. Points of application can only be found in everyday life and in the aspirations, desires, ambitions, fears and values which shape that everyday life.

The 'everyday' is nothing new as a source of inspiration for architecture and urbanism. Architecture dating from just after the Second World War has recently become the object a renewed interest, the rediscovery of the work by the Smithsons, for example, is proof of that. The consideration for the everyday threads like an intermittent sidebar through the history of the social sciences, the arts and philosophy, from Walter Benjamin via Georg Simmel, surrealism, the Mass-Observation project in England, Henri Lefebvre and the situationists to Michel de Certeau.[2]

Throughout the history of theoretical reflection on daily life, different approaches have struggled to take the foreground. The main contention is still an issue today: should the engagement with the everyday take the form of a socio-pedagogical project (as a component in the emancipation of specific groups) or should it contain the whiff of liberation (the separation of life-world and the system)? This controversy is currently alive, for example in the debate about the policy for postwar neighbourhoods, in which concepts such as integration and values and norms predominate, in the face of an upswing in uncomplicated populism, traits of which are evident in the International Building Exhibition Rotterdam-Hoogvliet, which took the theme 'Welcome into My Backyard!' – 'WiMBY!' Neither view makes it impossible to see daily life for what it actually is. The quest for points of application in the everyday is constantly in danger of falling into that trap. The quotidian is not a homogeneous phenomenon, but one that is highly differentiated.

The way in which people organize their everyday lives is the resultant of a complex weighing-up of often-conflicting dreams and aspirations. Besides the various orientations of value systems which are currently receiving much attention in all kinds of lifestyle studies, the practical limitations and dilemmas – associated, for example, with the income and the composition of the household but also with family ties and friendships – also play a role in this. A specific 'world' with spatial, physical, social and cultural characteristics fits the resulting way of life. That way of life is certainly also determined by notions of distinction and reputation. In these worlds, familiarity and surprise, tradition and renewal, play a role alongside each other. Today's societal diversity is the result of the coexistence of different worlds with distinct notions of time and space. And these worlds are in flux rather than static. That distinguishes the modernity in which we live, the 'liquid modernity',[3] from the 'fixed modernity' of the not too distant past.

For a study into this fluid and plural everyday we can turn to George Perec for inspiration (besides sociologists such as Pierre Bourdieu and Michel de Certeau), who has elevated observing and describing everyday life to an art. He sometimes suffered heroically, as with the project for which he resolved to visit 12 places in Paris for 12 consecutive years, one each month, and to describe what he saw there. He also intended to describe these same 12 places at the same intervals based on his memory of them. That would have produced a total of $144 + 144 = 288$ descriptions.[4] The project proved overly ambitious even for Perec (who wrote a novel without once using the letter 'e') and eventually resulted in 'only' 133 descriptions. In that respect it resembles the prewar Mass-Observation project in England, which collated material from countless 'normal' correspondents about every aspect of everyday life (sounds, smells, food, clothing, household articles, advertisements, newspapers, etc.), but which failed equally heroically. However, just like the Perec project, the ambition is not in the project's scale, but in the endeavour to devise a method to understand the diverse and fluid everyday reality in a different way:
'Observe the street, from time to time, with some concern for system perhaps.
Apply yourself. Take your time.
Note down the place: the terrace of a café near the junction of the rue du Bac and the Boulevard Saint-Germain
the time : seven o'clock in the evening
the date : 15 May 1973
the weather : set fair.
Note down what you can see. Anything worthy of note going on. Do you know how to see what's really worthy of note? Is there anything that strikes you?
Nothing strikes you. You don't know how to see.
You must set about it more slowly, almost stupidly. Force yourself to write what is of no interest, what is most obvious, the most common, most colourless.'[5]

These are attempts to describe daily life in all its diversity – which necessarily led to experiments with the writing, a form of writing that, just like the architecture of Rietveld, does not want to fix and frame, which is apologetic and sometimes just as incidental as the things being described.

Does this lead anywhere? Perhaps. Maybe it leads to the discovery of the importance of the rosebushes which elevated the environment of the postwar neighbourhoods just above the level of the everyday, and which were later mercilessly cut down to be replaced by low-maintenance grass with no consideration for the role they played for the residents in terms of reputation and distinction. Or the social complexity that a staircase in such a neighbourhood imposes on the diverse residents, for which an architectural variant of the Berlin key might offer a solution. Or the differences in use and meaning that are associated with the various different forms of public space , the street, the square, the public garden and the park. Why do people want to leave behind 'those narrow streets' in the old neighbourhoods? Why is it perfectly natural to lie half-naked on the grass in a park, while it would be considered undesirable behaviour and a nuisance on a square? How is it possible that a few cubic metres of sand in Rotterdam can transform an empty quayside into a beach or that a couple of sods of turf are sufficient to change a square in Nijmegen into a park, bringing with them the attendant behavioural patterns?

Professional involvement – call it engagement if you will – entails a fascination for such remarkable scenarios. Architects and urbanists could thus develop an eye for the spatial and physical conditions which make it possible to live in urban environments, in other words: live together in high densities in the midst of people from different roots, backgrounds and perspectives. Assuming that there are enough people who desire this, and not because they feel morally obliged but because it coincides with their aspirations. Stacking stones then? Yes, that too. The professional task of architects and urbanist is not to become tied down by programmes but to create …. Architects and urbanists have the task of avoiding becoming stuck in thinking in programmes, and instead to create space that speaks for itself for the fluid and plural everyday.

Notes

1   Bruno Latour, 'The Berlin key or how to do words with things', in: P.M. Graves-Brown (ed.), Matter, Materiality and Modern Culture, Routledge, London and New York 2000, pp. 10-21.

2   See Ben Highmore, *Everyday Life and Cultural Theory. An Introduction* Routledge, London/New York 2002.

3   Zygmunt Bauman, *Liquid Modernity*, Polity Press, Cambridge 2000.

4   Bruno Latour, 'Paris – Perec' in *AA Files* 45/46 (Architectural Association, London, winter 2001).

5   George Perec, *Species of Space and Other Pieces*, trans. and ed. John Sturrock, Penguin, London/New York 1997.

The authors

Hans Aarsman is a photographer and author. His publications include *Hollandse Taferelen* (1989), an account of his journey through the Netherlands in a dormomobile; *Aarsmans Amsterdam* (1993), a sketch of his home city; and *Vrrooom! Vrrooom!* (2003) about his fascination with cars.

Aaron Betsky is director of the Netherlands Architecture Institute in Rotterdam. His most recent books are *Architecture Must Burn* (2000), and *Landscrapers* (2002). His *False Flat: Why Dutch Design Matters* will be published in 2003.

Jeroen Boomgaard is Reader in Art and Public Space at the Gerrit Rietveld Academy and the University of Amsterdam. He published *The magnetic era. Video art in the Netherlands 1970-1985* with Bart Rutten in 2003. He also published *Als de kunst er om vraagt; de Sonsbeektentoonstellingen van 1971, 1986 en 1993* with Marga van Mechelen and Miriam van Rijsingen in 2001.

René Boomkens is Professor of Social and Cultural Philosophy at the University of Groningen. He is founder and editor of *Krisis*, journal for empirical philosophy, and of the cultural monthly *De Gids*. He publishes regularly in several cultural and academic journals, including *Kennis & Methode, De Gids, Justitiële Verkenningen, Stedebouw & Ruimtelijke Ordening,* and *De Groene Amsterdammer*. His Ph.D. thesis *Een Drempelwereld. Moderne ervaring en stedelijke openbaarheid* was published in 1998. His *De verdwaalde voyeur. Globalisering, identiteit en alledaags leven* will be published in 2004.

Ole Bouman is editor-in-chief of *Archis. magazine for architecture, city and visual culture*. He is the author of *The Invisible in Architecture* (with Roemer van Toorn, 1994), *Rotterdam 2045* (1995), *Architecture on the Edge of Two Millennia* (1998), and *Time Wars* (2003).

Lieven De Cauter lectures in Architecture, Urban Design and Spatial Planning at the Catholic University Leuven and in Cultural Philosophy at the RITS film academy and the Berlage Institute in Rotterdam. His publications include *Het hiernamaals van de kunst* (1991), *Archeologie van de kick. Verhalen over moderniteit en ervaring* (1995), and *De Dwerg in de schaakautomaat. Benjamins* *verborgen leer* (1999). He co-authored *Dat is architectuur. Sleutel-teksten uit de twintigste eeuw* (2001).

Chris Dercon was director of Museum Boijmans Van Beuningen in Rotterdam from 1996-2003. As of 1 May 2003 he has been appointed director of the Haus der Kunst in Munich.

José van Dijck is Professor of Television, Media and Culture at the University of Amsterdam and chair of the Media Studies Department of the Faculty of Humanities of the same university.

Fred Feddes writes on spatial planning, landscape, architecture, cultural history and related topics.

Hans den Hartog Jager is an art critic for the *NRC Handelsblad*. He regularly writes texts for art books and published his first novel, *Zelf God worden*, in the spring of 2003.

Bas Heijne is associated with the *NRC Handelsblad* as an author and essayist. His publications include the collections of essays *De wijde wereld* (2000) and *Het verloren land* (2003), and the play *Van Gogh* (2003).

Hilde Heynen is Professor of Architectural Theory at the Catholic University Leuven. She is the author of *Architecture and Modernity: A Critique* (1999), and co-edited *Back from Utopia. The Challenge of the Modern Movement* with Hubert-Jan Henket in 2002.

H.J.A. Hofland works for the *NRC Handelsblad* as a columnist and journalist. His most recent publications are *Op zoek naar de pool* (2002) and *Het voorgekookt bestaan* (2002).

Hans Ibelings is an architecture critic and has written several books published by NAi Publishers. Recent titles are *The artificial landscape* (2000), *20th Century Dutch architecture* (2003), *ING Group Headquarters* (2003), and *Contemporary Traditionalism* (due to appear in December 2003).

Allard Jolles is a historian of architecture. Since 1991 he has been working as Coordinator of Professional Development at the Department of Spatial Planning in Amsterdam. He writes regularly for the website of ArchiNed and the daily *Cobouw* on architecture, urban planning, art and photography. He has collaborated on books about IJburg and the Eastern Harbour District in Amsterdam (2003).

Rudi Laermans is Full Professor in the Department of Sociology of the Faculty of Social Sciences of the Catholic University Leuven. He researches and regularly publishes on social systems theory, cultural policy and cultural theory, and the sociology of art.

Dieter Lesage is a philosopher and lecturer in the Department for Audiovisual and Dramatic Arts RITS, Erasmus University Brussels. His publications include *Namen als gezichten. Essay over de faam* (1996) and *Zwarte gedachten. Over België* (1998). He co-edited *Het museum van de natie. Van kolonialisme tot globalisering* (1999) with Herman Asselberghs.

Arjen Mulder is a biologist and essayist. His recent publications are *Boek voor de elektronische kunst* (with Maaike Post, 2000), *Levende systemen* (2002), and *Information is Alive* (co-edited with Joke Brouwer, 2003).

Rutger Pontzen is art editor for *de Volkskrant*. NAi Publishers published his *Nice! Towards a new form of commitment in art* in 2000.

Arnold Reijndorp is a freelance researcher on the interface between urban planning and urban culture. His recent publications are *Buitenwijk. Stedelijkheid op afstand* (co-authored, 1998), *In search of new public domain* (co-authored with Maarten Hajer, 2001) and *Stadswijk. Stedenbouw en dagelijks leven* (to be published in the spring of 2004).

Janny Rodermond has been director of the Architectural Promotion Fund since November 2002. She worked with the professional journal *de Architect* from 1979 to 2002, and was appointed editor-in-chief in 1995.

Gert Staal was editor-in-chief of *Items, design en visual communication* until recently. Before that he was deputy director of the Design Institute in Amsterdam. He has published many books in the field of design and architecture, such as *Holland in Vorm. Vormgeving in Nederland 1945-1987* (ed., 1987), and *IN side OUT / ON site IN. Redesigning the Netherlands Museum of Ethnology* (2003).

Anna Tilroe is an art critic and writer. She publishes in various media, including the *NRC-Handelsblad,* and has written three books of criticism and reflections on art, architecture, and the vision of the New Man and the New World.

Ton Verstegen is a journalist and writer. He is a member of staff of the Academy of Architecture in Arnhem.

Lucas Verweij is domain manager for Premsela, Foundation for Netherlands Design.
Ton Matton is an independent urban planner in Wendorf, Germany, and operates under the name Mattonoffice. Verweij and Matton established Buro Schie (later Schie 2.0) in 1991.

Acknowledgements

We are especially grateful to the following for their contribution to
the publication of the present volume: the Netherlands Architecture
Fund and the Mondriaan Foundation for subsidies to cover the
authors' fees and translation costs, and to Drukkerij Die Keure in
Bruges, Arctic Paper in Oud-Heverlee and Splichal Bookbinders in
Turnhout for their considerable contribution towards the cost of
production.

Editing: NAi Publishers
Text editing: NAi Publishers and Els Brinkman
Translations:
Pierre Bouvier (Dercon, Laermans, Staal)
Nancy Forest-Flier (Tilroe)
Lynn George (den Hartog Jager, Pontzen)
Joost den Haan/De Twee Hanen (Feddes)
Robyn de Jong-Dalziel (Bouman, Ibelings, Jolles, Mulder)
Peter Mason (Boomgaard, Heijne, Heynen, Rodermond, Verstegen)
Andrew May (Aarsman, Boomkens, Van Dijck, Reijndorp, Verweij)
Wendy van Os (Hofland, Lesage)
Arthur Payman (Betsky, De Cauter)
Proofreading: Pierre Bouvier
Copyright cover photograph: Reuters
Production: Barbera van Kooij, NAi Publishers
Publisher: Simon Franke, NAi Publishers
Design: Joseph Plateau Grafisch Ontwerpers, Amsterdam
Printing: Drukkerij Die Keure, Bruges
Binding: Splichal n.v., Turnhout
Printed on: Munken Lynx 115 grs. by Arctic Paper –
www.arcticpaper.com

NAi Publishers is an internationally orientated publisher specialized
in developing, producing and distributing books on architecture,
visual arts and related disciplines.
www.naipublishers.nl
info@naipublishers.nl

Available in North, South and Central America through D.A.P./
Distributed Art Publishers Inc, 155 Sixth Avenue 2nd Floor,
New York, NY 10013-1507, Tel 212 6271999, Fax 212 6279484.

Available in the United Kingdom and Ireland through Art Data, 12
Bell Industrial Estate, 50 Cunnington Street, London W4 5HB,
Tel 208 7471061, Fax 208 7422319.

Printed and bound in Belgium

ISBN 90-5662-347-8